Modern Critical Views

Edward Albee
Maya Angelou
Asian-American
 Writers
Margaret Atwood
Jane Austen
James Baldwin
Samuel Beckett
Saul Bellow
The Bible
William Blake
Jorge Luis Borges
Ray Bradbury
The Brontës
Gwendolyn Brooks
Robert Browning
Italo Calvino
Albert Camus
Lewis Carroll
Willa Cather
Cervantes
Geoffrey Chaucer
Anton Chekhov
Kate Chopin
Agatha Christie
Samuel Taylor
 Coleridge
Joseph Conrad
Contemporary Poets
Stephen Crane
Dante
Daniel Defoe
Charles Dickens
Emily Dickinson
John Donne and the
 17th-Century
 Poets
Fyodor Dostoevsky
W. E. B. DuBois
George Eliot
T. S. Eliot
Ralph Ellison
Ralph Waldo
 Emerson
William Faulkner
F. Scott Fitzgerald

Sigmund Freud
Robert Frost
George Gordon,
 Lord Byron
Graham Greene
Thomas Hardy
Nathaniel
 Hawthorne
Ernest Hemingway
Hispanic-American
 Writers
Homer
Langston Hughes
Zora Neale Hurston
Henrik Ibsen
John Irving
Henry James
James Joyce
Franz Kafka
John Keats
Jamaica Kincaid
Stephen King
Rudyard Kipling
D. H. Lawrence
Ursula K. Le Guin
Sinclair Lewis
Bernard Malamud
Christopher Marlowe
Gabriel García
 Márquez
Carson McCullers
Herman Melville
Arthur Miller
John Milton
Toni Morrison
Native-American
 Writers
Joyce Carol Oates
Flannery O'Connor
Eugene O'Neill
George Orwell
Sylvia Plath
Edgar Allan Poe
Katherine Anne
 Porter
J. D. Salinger

Jean-Paul Sartre
William Shakespeare:
 Histories and
 Poems
William Shakespeare's
 Romances
William Shakespeare:
 The Comedies
William Shakespeare:
 The Tragedies
George Bernard
 Shaw
Mary Wollstonecraft
 Shelley
Percy Bysshe Shelley
Alexander
 Solzhenitsyn
Sophocles
John Steinbeck
Tom Stoppard
Jonathan Swift
Amy Tan
Alfred, Lord
 Tennyson
Henry David
 Thoreau
J. R. R. Tolkien
Leo Tolstoy
Mark Twain
John Updike
Kurt Vonnegut
Alice Walker
Robert Penn Warren
Eudora Welty
Edith Wharton
Walt Whitman
Oscar Wilde
Tennessee Williams
Thomas Wolfe
Tom Wolfe
Virginia Woolf
William Wordsworth
Richard Wright
William Butler Yeats

Modern Critical Views

RAY BRADBURY

Edited and with an introduction by
Harold Bloom
Sterling Professor of the Humanities
Yale University

CHELSEA HOUSE PUBLISHERS
Philadelphia

Printed and bound in the United States of America

10 9 8 7 6 5 4 3 2

∞ The paper used in this publication meets the minimum
requirements of the American National Standard for
Permanence of Paper for Printed Library Materials,
Z39.48-1984

Library of Congress Cataloging-in-Publication Data

Ray Bradbury / edited by Harold Bloom.
    p. cm.
  Includes bibliographical references and index.
  ISBN 0-7910-5914-6
    1. Bradbury, Ray, 1920–   Criticism and interpretation.
2. Science fiction, American—History and criticism.
    I. Bloom, Harold.

  PS3503.R167 Z852 2000
  813'.54—dc21   00-022682

Chelsea House Publishers
1974 Sproul Road, Suite 400
Broomall, PA 19008-0914

The Chelsea House World Wide Web address is
http://www.chelseahouse.com

Contributing Editor: Tenley Williams

Contents

Editor's Note

My Introduction tries to evaluate the literary achievement of Bradbury by centering upon his well-known story "The Golden Apples of the Sun."

Damon Knight shrewdly analyzes Bradbury's subject as "childhood and the buried child-in-man," while Wayne L. Johnson studies Bradbury's stories in which our world is invaded by "mysterious creatures."

Bradbury himself sees science fiction as imagination returning to literature, a contention persuasive to those already persuaded, such as Wayne L. Johnson, who returns with an account of Bradbury's immensely popular *Martian Chronicles.*

In a reading that contrasts strongly with my Introduction, William F. Touponce discovers complexities and intellectual depths in "The Golden Apples of the Sun."

Gothic romance is seen as being rejuvenated in Bradbury by Hazel Pierce, after which Lahna Diskin brings us back to Bradbury's representations of children.

Frontier myth, persuasive in our country's culture, is chronicled in Bradbury's work by Gary K. Wolfe, while the Cold War is invoked as context for *Fahrenheit 451* and *The Martian Chronicles* by Kevin Hoskinson.

Introduction

Science fiction, despite its vast, worldwide audience still exists on the borderlands of imaginative literature. I am being sadly accurate, and hardly haughty. William F. Touponce, in his essay on Ray Bradbury's "The Golden Apples of the Sun," reprinted in this volume, cites the eminent critic Geoffrey H. Hartman as sharing in the French appreciation for Bradbury's achievement. One remembers that the French have exalted Jerry Lewis and Mickey Rourke as masters of cinema. Perhaps Hartman read Bradbury in French translation, since Bradbury, like Poe, improves in translation.

Bradbury indeed is one of the masters of science fiction and fantasy, and he is highly inventive and humane. His palpable failure is in style: his language is thin, and his characters are names upon the page. *Fahrenheit 451* and *The Martian Chronicles* lack the literary distinction of Ursula Le Guin's *The Left Hand of Darkness*, David Lindsay's *A Voyage to Arcturus*, and John Crowley's *Little, Big* and *Ægypt* series. But I enjoy reading Bradbury, once each, and have no case to urge against him. He writes popular fiction, like John Grisham and Michael Crichton, though his mode differs from theirs. At a time when all literary and aesthetic standards are collapsing, one urges a little perspective upon readers. Bradbury is an admirable entertainer, and deserves appreciation precisely as such.

Like many other readers, I judge Bradbury's best story to be "The Golden Apples of the Sun," a simplistic but winning allegory of Promethean quest. The rocket ship *Capa de Oro* (Cup of Gold) heads straight for the sun, in order to scoop up a chunk of that divine heat. Its captain is only barely characterized, but clearly he is the most benign of Center. He is no Ahab and the sun is not Moby-Dick. Ahab cried out that he would strike the sun if it insulted him, but Bradbury's captain regards the sun as an energy-field, not as an antagonist. This amiable thief of fire wishes only to bring home something that will burn endlessly, to human benefit.

To call "The Golden Apples of the Sun" a short story is to endanger it. You cannot read it side-by-side with Chekhov, Flannery O'Connor, Hemingway or Borges. It is a parable, and probably Bradbury is best thought of as a fabulist, a teller of moral tales. His morals tend to extrude, but doubtless he has done his audience much good, here and abroad. Like many other science fantasists, he is a belated apostle of the Enlightenment.

DAMON KNIGHT

When I Was in Kneepants: Ray Bradbury

Ray Bradbury began writing professionally at the floodtide of the cerebral story in science fiction—in 1940, when John Campbell was revolutionizing the field with a new respect for facts, and a wholly justified contempt for the overblown emotional values of the thirties. Bradbury, who had nothing but emotion to offer, couldn't sell Campbell.

Bradbury didn't care. He adapted his work just enough to meet the standards of the lesser markets—he filled it with the second-hand furniture of contemporary science fiction and fantasy—and went on writing what he chose.

It's curious to look back now on those first Bradbury stories and reflect how far they have brought their author. Not many of them are stories at all; most are intensely realized fragments, padded out with any handy straw. The substance of "The Next in Line," for one especially vivid example, is in a two-page description of some Mexican mummies, as relentlessly and embarrassingly horrible as any tourist photograph. The remainder—the two American visitors, the car trouble, the hotel room, the magazines—is not relevant, it merely plumps out the skeleton enough to get it into a conventional suit of clothes.

On a story-a-week schedule, Bradbury sold prodigiously to *Weird Tales, Planet Stories, Thrilling Wonder.* One day we awoke to discover that he had

From *In Search of Wonder: Essays on Modern Science Fiction.* Copyright © 1956, 1967 by Damon Knight.

leapfrogged over John Campbell's head, outside our microcosm altogether: his work was beginning to appear in *Harper's*; in *Mademoiselle*; in the *O. Henry Prize Stories*; on the radio; in *Esquire, Collier's, The Saturday Evening Post*.

Outside the huge, brightly-colored bubble he had blown around himself, "serious" critics reacted with rapture:

> . . . the sheer lift and power of a truly original imagination exhilarates . . . His is a very great and unusual talent.
>   —Christopher Isherwood

Inside the bubble, we get at once a clearer and a more distorted view of Bradbury. Although he has a large following among science fiction readers, there is at least an equally large contingent of people who cannot stomach his work at all; they say he has no respect for the medium; that he does not even trouble to make his scientific double-talk convincing; that—worst crime of all—he fears and distrusts science.

. . . All of which is true, and—for our present purposes, anyhow—irrelevant. The purists are right in saying that he does not write science fiction, and never has.

To Bradbury, as to most people, radar and rocket ships and atomic power are big, frightening, meaningless names: a fact which, no doubt, has something to do with his popular success, but which does not touch the root of the matter. Bradbury's strength lies in the fact that he writes about the things that are really important to us—not the things we pretend we are interested in—science, marriage, sports, politics, crime—but the fundamental prerational fears and longings and desires: the rage at being born; the will to be loved; the longing to communicate; the hatred of parents and siblings, the fear of things that are not self. . . .

People who talk about Bradbury's imagination miss the point. His imagination is mediocre; he borrows nearly all his backgrounds and props, and distorts them badly; wherever he is required to invent anything—a planet, a Martian, a machine—the image is flat and unconvincing. Bradbury's Mars, where it is not as bare as a Chinese stage-setting, is a mass of inconsistency; his spaceships are a joke; his people have no faces. The vivid images in his work are not imagined; they are remembered.

Here is the shock of birth, in "No Particular Night or Morning":

> "Have you talked about this to the psychiatrist?"
> "So he could try to mortar up the gaps for me, fill in the gulfs with noise and warm water and words and hands touching me . . . ?"

And the death-wish, Bradbury's most recurrent theme:

> . . . When I was living I was jealous of you, Lespere . . .
> Women frightened me and I went into space, always wanting
> them and jealous of you for having them, and money, and as
> much happiness as you could have in your own wild way. But
> now, falling here, with everything over, I'm not jealous of you
> any more, because it's over for you as it is for me, and right now
> it's like it never was. ("Kaleidoscope.")

> Forty-five thousand people killed every year on this conti-
> nent . . . made into jelly right in the can, as it were, in the auto-
> mobiles. Red blood jelly, with white marrow bones like sudden
> thoughts . . . The cars roll up in tight sardine rolls—all sauce,
> all silence.
> . . . You look out your window and see two people lying atop
> each other in friendly fashion who, a moment ago, had never met
> before, dead . . . ("The Concrete Mixer.")

The gulf between Bradbury and the science fiction writers is nowhere
more clearly evident than in the lavish similes and metaphors that are his
trademarks:

> The first concussion cut the rocket up the side with a giant
> can opener. The men were thrown into space like a dozen wrig-
> gling silverfish. ("Kaleidoscope.")

> . . . And here were the lions now . . . so feverishly and star-
> tlingly real that you could feel the prickling fur on your hand,
> and your mouth was stuffed with the dusty upholstery smell of
> their heated pelts . . . ("The Veldt.")

The aim of science-fantasy, more and more as it becomes what it has
always tried to be—adult fiction—is to expand the imagination, stretch it to
include things never before seen or dreamed of. Bradbury's subject is childhood and the buried child-in-man; his aim is to narrow the focus, not to
widen it; to shrink all the big frightening things to the compass of the
familiar: a spaceship to a tin can; a Fourth of July rocket to a brass kettle; a
lion to a Teddy bear.

There is so much to say about Bradbury's meaning that perhaps too
little has been said about his technique. He is a superb craftsman, a man who

has a great gift and has spent fifteen years laboriously and with love teaching himself to use it. "For here was a kind of writing of which there is never much in any one time—a style at once delicate, economical and unobtrusively firm, sharp enough to cut but without rancor, and clear as water or air." That's Stephen Vincent Benét, writing in 1938 about Robert Nathan; the same words, all but the next to last phrase, might have been written with equal justice of Bradbury. His imagery is luminous and penetrating, continually lighting up familiar corners with unexpected words. He never lets an idea go until he has squeezed it dry, and never wastes one. I well remember my own popeyed admiration when I read his story about a woman who gave birth to a small blue pyramid; this is exactly the sort of thing that might occur to any imaginative writer in a manic or drunken moment; but Bradbury wrote it and sold it.

Why Bradbury's world-line and that of the animated cartoon have never intersected, I do not know; perhaps because the result would necessarily scare the American theater-going public out of its underpants; but clearly, in such stories as "Jack-in-the-Box," Bradbury is writing for no other medium. The gaudy colors and plush textures, the dream-swift or dream-slow motion, the sudden dartings into unsuspected depths of perspective, or contrariwise, the ballooning of a face into the foreground—these are all distinctive techniques of the animated cartoon, and Bradbury uses them all.

As for the rancor, the underlying motif of much early Bradbury, the newer stories show little of it; this might be taken as a sign that Bradbury is mellowing in his thirties, and perhaps he is; I have the feeling that he is rather trying to mellow—deliberately searching for something equally strong, equally individual, less antagonistic toward the universe that buys his stories. I don't think he has yet found it. There's the wry, earthy humor of "En la Noche," the pure fancy of "The Golden Kite, The Silver Wind"; these are neutral stories, anyone might have written them. There are the moralistic tales; if you find the moral palatable, as I do in "The Big Black and White Game" and "Way in the Middle of the Air," these are sincere and moving; if you don't, as I don't in "Powerhouse" or "The Fire Balloons," there is a pious flatness about them. Then there is sentiment; and since Bradbury does nothing by halves, it is sentiment that threatens continually to slop over into sentimentality. At its precarious peak, it is a moving and vital thing: when it slops, it is—no other word will do—sickening.

It has been said of Bradbury that, like H. P. Lovecraft, he was born a century or so too late. I think he would have been a castaway in any age; if he would like to destroy airplanes, television sets, automatic washing machines, it's not because they make loud noises or because they have no faces or even because some of them kill people, but because they are grown-up things; because they symbolize the big, loud, faceless, violent, unromantic world of adults.

Childhood is after all Bradbury's one subject. When he writes of grown-up explorers visiting the sun or the Jurassic jungles, they are palpably children playing at spacemen or time-travelers. He writes feelingly and with sharp perception of young women and of old people—because, I think, he finds them childlike. But it's only when the theme becomes explicit that his song sings truest:

> The boys were playing on the green park diamond when he came by. He stood a little while among the oak-tree shadows, watching them hurl the white, snowy baseball into the warm summer air, saw the baseball shadow fly like a dark bird over the grass, saw their hands open in mouths to catch this swift piece of summer that now seemed most especially important to hold onto. . . .
>
> How tall they stood to the sun. In the last few months it seemed the sun had passed a hand above their heads, beckoned, and they were warm metal drawn melting upwards; they were golden taffy pulled by an immense gravity to the sky, thirteen, fourteen years old, looking down upon Willie, smiling, but already beginning to neglect him . . .

Learned opinion to the contrary, Bradbury is not the heir of Poe, Irving or Hawthorne; his voice is the voice (a little shriller) of Christopher Morley and Robert Nathan and J. D. Salinger. As his talent expands, some of his stories become pointed social commentary; some are surprisingly effective religious tracts, disguised as science fiction; others still are nostalgic vignettes; but under it all is still Bradbury the poet of 20th-century neurosis, Bradbury the isolated spark of consciousness, awake and alone at midnight; Bradbury the grown-up child who still remembers, still believes.

The young Ray Bradbury wrote a story called "Skeleton," about a man obsessed by the fact that he carries a horrid, white, grinning skeleton inside him. The story was raw, exuberant, gauche, pretentious, insulting to the intellect, and unforgettable. *Weird Tales* published it, and later it appeared in Bradbury's first collection, *Dark Carnival.*

The story did not soothe its readers' anxieties nor pamper their prejudices, nor provide vicarious adventure in a romantic setting. Far from solving his problem by his own courage and resourcefulness, the hero let it be solved for him by a strange little man named Munigant, who crawled down his throat, gnawed, crunched and munched away the bones which had so annoyed him, and left him lying on his carpet, a human jellyfish.

Time passed; Bradbury got a little older, stopped running quite so hard. His stories acquired depth, smoothness, polish. Little by little he stopped writing about corpses, vampires, cemeteries, things in jars; instead he wrote about civil rights, religion and good home cooking. The slicks, which had begun buying him as a curiosity when he was horrid, kept on buying him as a staple when he turned syrupy.

Dandelion Wine consists of sixteen loosely connected tales without a ghost or a goblin in them; they are familiar in tone and rhythm, but these stories are no longer what we mean by fantasy; they are what Hollywood means by fantasy. The setting is an imaginary Midwestern town, seen through the wrong end of a rose-colored glass. The period is as vague as the place; Bradbury calls it 1928, but it has no feeling of genuine recollection; most of the time it is like second-hand 1910.

Childhood is Bradbury's one subject, but you will not find real childhood here, Bradbury's least of all. What he has had to say about it has always been expressed obliquely, in symbol and allusion, and always with the tension of the outsider—the ex-child, the lonely one. In giving up this tension, in diving with arms spread into the glutinous pool of sentimentality that has always been waiting for him, Bradbury has renounced the one thing that made him worth reading.

All the rest is still here: the vivid images, the bombardment of tastes and sounds and smells; the clipped, faceless prose; the heavy nostalgia, the cuteness, the lurking impudence. The phrases, as before, are poignant ("with the little gray toad of a heart flopping weakly here or there in his chest") or silly to the point of self-parody ("lemon-smelling men's room"). The characters are as lifelike as Bradbury's characters ever were: bright, pert, peppermint-stick people, epicene, with cotton-candy hair and sugar smiles.

Maybe Bradbury, like his own protagonist in "Skeleton," grew uneasy about the macabre forces in himself: or maybe success, that nemesis of American writers, was Bradbury's M. Munigant. Whatever the reason, the skeleton has vanished; what's left is recognizable but limp.

WAYNE L. JOHNSON

The Invasion Stories of Ray Bradbury

Seven-year-old Mink bursts into the house and begins snatching up kitchen utensils and apparently random bits of junk to be hauled outside for use in some mysterious game. "What's the name of the game?" inquires her mother. "Invasion!" the girl replies. Mink's mother goes on about her housework unaware that her daughter is telling the literal truth, and that what appears to be an innocent children's game is actually the prelude to an invasion of Earth by creatures from another world—Ray Bradbury style.

The theme of invasion is one of the oldest in science fiction. The early idea that other planets might be inhabited quite naturally suggested the possibility of eventual contact between our world and another. If the theory of evolution were correct, then it was conceivable that life forms on other planets had begun evolving thousands, even million of years before those on Earth. Intelligent beings on Mars, for instance, might already be technologically advanced enough to visit Earth. Should they decide to do so, wouldn't their very advancement prove a threat to us?

H. G. Wells's book *The War of the Worlds* (1898) answered the question with a very dramatic yes. Wells's Martians—cold, emotionless, octopuslike horrors—fled their own dying planet and sought to conquer Earth, exterminating most of the human race in the process. The elements of the story were classic, and formed the basis for countless Earth vs. Alien tales. Science

From *Critical Encounters: Writers and Themes in Science Fiction.* © 1978 by Frederick Ungar Publishing Co., Inc.

fiction pulp magazines entered a phase of greatly increased popularity during the first half of the twentieth century. The two World Wars, with their immense firepower and destructiveness, created an atmosphere quite sympathetic to stories of interplanetary invasion and warfare. In America, Orson Welles's 1938 documentary-style radio version of *The War of the Worlds* was so realistic it caused a panic, and brought the idea of interplanetary invasion to general public consciousness.

Because of the dramatic possibilities of the subject, invasion became a popular theme in science fiction film and television productions. For instance, when Bradbury's short story "The Fog Horn" was made into a film, it was drastically altered to include an invasion motif. Thus Bradbury's rather touching story of a lonely ocean-dwelling dinosaur who mistakes a lighthouse foghorn for the cry of a long-lost mate became "The Beast from 20,000 Fathoms," in which a typical Hollywood monster charges ashore and demolishes large sections of New York City.

Bradbury has written a number of real invasion stories, of course, and these fall into two main groups: those that involve the invasion of Earth by aliens, and those that involve the invasion of Mars by Earthmen. The story about Mink and her mother belongs in the first group. It's called "Zero Hour," and comes from the collection of Bradbury's stories entitled *The Illustrated Man.* "Zero Hour" is essentially a suspense story. Mink's mother, Mrs. Morris, watches her daughter and the other young children in the neighborhood as they dart about playing their little game. As the day progresses, the game takes on some disturbing overtones. Mink and her friends appear to be talking to an unseen playmate in the rose bush, whom they address as Drill. When Mrs. Morris questions her daughter about this, the girl freely admits that Drill is an alien being from another dimension who is telepathically instructing the children. The aliens are teaching the children to build machines that will allow them to break through from their dimension into ours. The aliens know that no adult will take the children's game seriously until it is too late. This, of course, includes Mrs. Morris. Mink complains that some of the older boys have been teasing her and her friends: "They're so snooty, 'cause they're growing up. You'd think they'd know better. They were little only a coupla years ago. I hate them worst. We'll kill them *first.*" To this Mrs. Morris is mildly patronizing. Half jokingly she asks if parents are to be killed too. Without hesitation, Mink answers that they are: "Drill says you're dangerous. Know why? 'Cause you don't believe in Martians. They're going to let us run the world. Well, not just us, but kids over in the next block too. I might be queen."

Our realization that Mink means business comes early in the story. We wait to see how long it will take Mrs. Morris to catch on, but we know the mother is essentially a helpless figure. What Mink says about her and other adults is true. Even if Mrs. Morris could accept her daughter's story, we know she would not be able to convince other adults. In any case, the idea is just too fantastic. At five o'clock, the previously announced "zero hour," Mr. Morris arrives home from work. Suddenly there is a loud buzzing outside, followed by explosions. Mrs. Morris realizes the truth. She drags her astonished husband up into the attic and locks the door. Heavy footsteps mount the stairs, the lock on the attic door melts and the door swings open. A smiling Mink peers in, tall blue shadows visible behind her, and ends the story by saying "Peekaboo."

"Zero Hour" derives much of its impact from its quiet suburban setting. Mrs. Morris's life is calm, well-ordered, secure. There is considerable irony in the fact that it is not the child's imagination that dominates the scene, but rather Mrs. Morris's fantasy of her own secure suburban life. This fantasy is so strong that the mother weaves all of her daughter's increasingly threatening remarks into it. Mink is only playing a game as all children do—isn't that reassuring? Mink, on the other hand, is not imagining things at all. She sees the facts quite clearly and, at least as far as Drill allows her to, she sees through her mother's illusions.

Aliens take advantage of a quiet suburban setting again in "Boys! Raise Giant Mushrooms in *Your* Cellar!" from the collection *The Machineries of Joy*. This time the protagonist is one Hugh Fortnum. Fortnum looks out his window one bright Saturday morning and notices his next door neighbor, Mrs. Goodbody, spraying great clouds of insecticide in all directions. He asks her what the trouble is.

"What would you say," she asks, "if I told you I was the first line of defense concerning flying saucers?"

Fortnum humors her. "Fine . . . There'll be rockets between the worlds any year now."

"'There already *are!*' She pumped, aiming the spray under the hedge. 'There! Take that!'"

A few minutes later, a special delivery package arrives for Fortnum's son Tom. Inspired by an ad in *Popular Mechanics*, Tom had sent away for a box of "Sylvan Glade Jumbo-Giant Guaranteed Growth Raise-Them-in-Your-Cellar-for-Big-Profit Mushrooms." Almost immediately, Tom disappears down into the cellar to begin raising his crop. In a plot essentially the same as "Zero Hour," it is Hugh Fortnum's fate to have an invasion plot unfold before his eyes while we wait to see if he will put the pieces of the puzzle together in time. The development of the story is more diffuse than in "Zero Hour," because, for one thing, Fortnum is not alone in uncovering the invasion. There is Mrs. Goodbody—though she does not seem aware of events outside her own garden—and there is Roger Willis. Willis flags down Fortnum later in the morning when Fortnum is driving to the store. Once in the car, Willis immediately begins complaining of an unexplainable feeling he has that "something's wrong with the world." Willis has no hard evidence to pin his anxiety on: "Maybe there's something wrong with the way the wind blows these weeds there in the lot. Maybe it's the sun up on those telephone wires or the cicadas singing in the elm trees. If only we could stop, look, listen, a few days, a few nights, and compare notes."

Fortnum asks what they should be looking for, and Willis replies, "You'll know. You've got to know. Or we're done for, all of us."

By evening, Fortnum has guessed that the Earth is being invaded and that the mushrooms are somehow involved. When he tells this to his wife, she laughs. How, she asks, could mushrooms without even arms or legs take over the world? Fortnum has no answer. After his wife has gone upstairs to bed, Fortnum goes to the refrigerator for a snack. There, on a shelf in the refrigerator, is a bowl of freshly cut mushrooms. At last comes the crucial realization: The mushrooms infiltrate the human body through the stomach; once he has eaten a mushroom, a human being *becomes* an alien.

Fortnum hears his son working down in the cellar. He calls out to the boy and asks if by any chance he has eaten any of the mushrooms. In a cold, faint voice, Tom replies that he has. Tom then asks his father to come down into the cellar to view the crop. Fortnum knows that by now millions of boys have raised billions of mushrooms around the world. As he stands at the top of the cellar stairs, Fortnum struggles with the incredibility of what he knows to be true: "He looked back at the stair leading up to his wife. I suppose, he thought, I should go say goodbye to Cynthia. But why should I think that! Why, in God's name, should I think that at all? No reason, *is* there?" Fortnum then steps down into the darkened cellar, closing the door behind him.

Since "Zero Hour" and "Mushrooms" are both primarily suspense stories, they share a number of structural traits common to such stories. For instance, the secret of the invasion is revealed to the reader almost at once. Real-life invasions usually depend heavily upon the element of surprise—such as in the attack on Pearl Harbor or in the invasion of Normandy. But in a story it is difficult to sustain reader interest if the main point is concealed until the very end. By revealing the invaders' intentions at the beginning of the story, Bradbury keeps us in constant suspense, wondering if and when the protagonists will catch on. In both stories, the method of invasion is rather improbable. This is necessary because the main character must be teasingly slow in putting the pieces of the puzzle together—but without coming off as an idiot. Because the invaders' plans are quite far-fetched, we can understand it when the main characters rationalize away the threat on the basis of its incredibility and their own need to live in a safe world where such things do not happen.

Both "Zero Hour" and "Mushrooms" focus on a small area. Though the invasions are on a world-wide scale, we see little of what is happening outside the neighborhood of the main characters. An even tighter focus is maintained in the story "Fever Dream" from *A Medicine for Melancholy*. Here again an invasion of Earth by mysterious creatures is taking place. But this time only one person knows, and there is no way he can tell anyone else about it, for the invasion is taking place within his own body.

Thirteen-year-old Charles has been put to bed with what seems to be a bad cold. From the outside, it seems like nothing more. But Charles has begun to experience strange symptoms, which he tries to communicate to his doctor: "My *hand*, it doesn't *belong* to me any more. This morning it *changed* into something else. I want you to change it back, Doctor, Doctor!" Charles's hand shows no external signs of change, and the doctor treats the matter lightly—"You just had a little fever dream." He gives Charles a pill and leaves.

> At four o'clock his other hand changed. It seemed almost to become a fever. It pulsed and shifted, cell by cell. It beat like a warm heart. The fingernails turned blue and then red. It took about an hour for it to change and when it was finished, it looked just like any ordinary hand. But it was not ordinary. It no longer was him any more.

Cut off from his disbelieving parents and the doctor, Charles tries to understand what is happening to him. He recalls how, in a book he once read, ancient trees became petrified as their wood cells were replaced by minerals. On the outside they still looked like trees, but in reality they had changed to stone.

"What would happen," Charles later asks the doctor, if "a lot of microbes got together and wanted to make a bunch, and reproduced and made *more*. . . . And they decided to *take over* a person!" Indeed, Charles has hit upon the truth, but even as he speaks his hands—possessed of a life of their own—crawl up his chest to his throat and begin to strangle him.

Later, alone again, and with his hands strapped to his legs, Charles submits to the progressive take-over of his body. He is trapped more completely than if surrounded by a whole army of soldiers. In a macabre parody of the old wives' cure for insomnia—wherein one relaxes his hands, then feet, then arms, then legs, until theoretically the entire body is relaxed—Charles's body is taken away from him bit by bit. Finally only his head is left, and in silent panic he feels his ears go deaf, his eyes go blind, and "his brain fill with a boiling mercury."

This story is a reversal of the previous stories in which the invaders were, at least in the beginning, external to the victims and brought about an internal psychological struggle. In "Fever Dream," the invasion begins with one person, and after it has conquered him, it moves out into the world at large. Bradbury only touches upon this second phase as Charles, suddenly appearing well again, goes to great lengths to get into physical contact with his parents, the doctor, even his pet parakeet. We realize that Charles is now one of the invaders—a carrier—and is eagerly involved in spreading the invasion. We know too that there will be no clash of armies or weaponry, just the futile struggle of one individual after another with his or her fever dream.

The novel *Something Wicked This Way Comes* is in many ways a novel about invasion. In this case, not about an attack by extraterrestrial aliens, but about the invasion of a small American town by forces of darkness and evil. The story takes place in Green Town, Illinois, setting for many Bradbury short stories as well as the novel *Dandelion Wine*, and roughly patterned after Bradbury's home town of Waukegan, Illinois.

Green Town is invaded by Cooger and Dark's Pandemonium Shadow Show—on the surface a carnival, but in reality a collection of magicians, witches, and evil-doers long banished from modern society, who come to exercise their powers on Halloween, the one night when they can again hold sway over the Earth. Only two boys and a middle-aged man are aware of the true nature of the carnival, and it falls upon them to repel the invasion. The boys are aptly suited for a battle with magic. Both were born on Halloween— James Nightshade at one minute after midnight, and William Halloway at one minute before. The adult is Charles Halloway, Will's father, the janitor at the public library, a boy who never grew up.

The threat faced by these three is more subtle than an armed military invasion. Because belief in magic, superstition, and fear are individual matters, the danger posed by the carnival is different for every person in town. The carnival draws people to itself by appealing to their unfulfilled needs, their selfishness and cruelty. It holds out to some people the promise of having their deepest wishes fulfilled, then enslaves them with their own greed. Thus the carnival provides itself with a steady supply of new freaks. Charles Halloway eventually realizes that Cooger and Dark's show draws all its energy from the fear and hatred it arouses in its victims, and this gives him the secret he needs to win out.

At the conclusion of *Something Wicked*, Dark, the carnival master, disguises himself as a young boy looking for help, and succeeds in luring

Halloway away from Will and Jim. Halloway quickly recognizes that Dark has tricked him to get him alone, but rather than struggle, Halloway suddenly embraces the astonished Dark. Halloway says to himself, "Evil has only the power we give it. I give you nothing. I take back. Starve. Starve. Starve." Without Halloway's fear and hatred to strengthen him, Dark shrivels away to nothing, and the invasion of Green Town comes to a quiet end.

It will be noted that children play important roles in the stories covered so far and in several of those to follow. Bradbury's use of children in general in his stories is too large a subject to treat here. But with respect to stories about invasion, Bradbury seems to agree with the popular concept that children live in a world of their own. Though they occupy the same space as adults do, their perception of it is, in many ways, radically different. They are, in a sense, aliens in their own world. In a story (not about invasion) from the book *Dark Carnival*, Bradbury has a rather paranoid school teacher say to his class, "Sometimes I actually believe that children are invaders from another dimension. . . . You are another race entirely, your motives, your beliefs, your disobediences. You are not human. You are—children." It may not be realistic to view the place of children in the world as in any way sinister, but in Bradbury's hands, it can certainly result in a good story.

Another common element in Bradbury's invasion stories is the theme of metamorphosis. In many stories, such as "Mushrooms" or "Fever Dream," the victim of the invasion undergoes—or prepares to undergo—a change in which he himself becomes one of the invaders. Bradbury frequently plays off of the ambiguity of the relationship between the invader and the invaded. At the moment an invasion succeeds, the invader becomes defender—capable himself of being invaded. In some of the stories about Mars, Earthmen who have begun living on Mars are faced with the fact that they are becoming, naturally enough, Martians. In some cases, the metamorphosis is literal, as in "Fever Dream," but behind this is the metaphorical truth that an invasion may be less of a change of circumstance than a change of mind.

Invasions succeed as often by the demoralization of the invaded as by the simple strength of the invaders. The means by which an invader travels can provide him with an important psychological advantage. In "Mushrooms" and "Fever Dream," Bradbury uses covert, Trojan Horse–type devices in which the invaders arrive in disguise and are not recognized for what they are until it is too late. In other stories, involving Mars and Earth, the invasion device is usually the commonplace but inevitable rocket ship. In *Something Wicked This Way Comes* the forces of evil arrive in a circus train.

Will and Jim witness the train's approach in the dead of night. They suspect that the train is bringing evil to their small town, and these suspicions are confirmed when they hear the train's dreadful whistle:

The wails of a lifetime were gathered in it from other nights in other slumbering years; the howl of moondreamed dogs, the seep of river-cold winds through the January porch screens which stopped the blood, a thousand fire sirens weeping, or worse! the outgone shreds of breath, the protests of a billion people dead or dying, not wanting to be dead, their groans, their sighs, burst over the earth!

Sometimes the mere presence of an alien force is enough to destroy a people's will to resist. In "Perhaps We Are Going Away," from *The Machineries of Joy*, an Indian boy, Ho-Awi, awakens to a day that is "evil for no reason." Ho-Awi belongs to a tribe named after a bird that lives near a mountain range named after the shadows of owls. Like the birds that are featured symbolically in their myths, the Indians of the tribe are sensitive to subtle disturbances in natural events.

In the hours before dawn, Ho-Awi joins his grandfather to hunt down the cause of the ominous feeling that pervades the air. They search for evidence that something is amiss in the natural world: "They scanned the prairies, but found only the winds which played there like tribal children all day." At length they approach the shore of the great eastern ocean and Ho-Awi's grandfather catches sight of something that confirms his worst fears. He tells Ho-Awi that a great change is coming, like a change of season. Though it is just the beginning of summer, birds that cannot be seen are flying south. "I feel them pass south in my blood. Summer goes. We may go with it." Ho-Awi asks if this course of things can be stopped or reversed, but the old man, who has already spotted the first encampment of white men on the beach, knows it cannot: "Not you or me or our people can stay this weather. It is a season changed, come to live on the land for all time."

Ho-Awi then sees the white men's camp himself, and realizes his grandfather is right. Not that there is much to see, just the glint of firelight on armor, a few faces, and out on the water "a great dark canoe with things like torn clouds hung on poles over it." But the metal and the ship are evidence of a vast technological gap. So intimidating is this gap that the two Indians who have seen the modest vanguard of the white man's invasion feel their entire world vanishing. There is no warning they can give that will prepare their tribe for what is to come. Physical resistance may eventually follow, but this will be to no avail, because the psychological battle has already been lost.

Hundreds of years later, in August of 1999, the planet Mars seems enveloped by a similarly disturbing atmosphere. In "The Summer Night," from *The Martian Chronicles*, strange thoughts pop into Martian heads as if from nowhere. In a theater, a Martian woman begins to sing words that are utterly alien to her: "She walks in beauty, like the night / Of cloudless climes and starry skys . . ." All over the planet, similar things occur. Children sing strange rhymes, lovers awaken humming unknown melodies. Women awake from violent nightmares and declare, "Something terrible will happen in the morning." The Martians try to reassure one another before settling into an uneasy sleep. The story ends with a lone night watchman patrolling empty streets and humming a very strange song.

Earthmen, who of course are on the way, do not appear at all in this story. But their presence has already invaded the minds of the telepathic Martians. The outcome of the coming invasion by Earthmen is not stated, but the fact that the Martians are already speaking our language, and find themselves frightened and dismayed by that fact implies that their fate will not be a happy one. The technological level of the Martians is not clear. They seem somewhat like ancient Greeks, attending concerts in marble amphitheaters while children play in torchlit alleys. There is mention of boats "as delicate as bronze flowers" drifting through canals, and of meals cooked on tables "where lava bubbled silvery and hushed." So the Martians obviously have some technological advancement. But the Martians seem to have made a decision about machinery, consigning it to a modest role in their society as an art form, a toy, and an unobtrusive support for a pastoral life style. Though it does not appear in this story, the very existence of a rocket ship en route from Earth to Mars suggests a technology out of sympathy with, and potentially destructive to, the Martian way of life.

We have come to the second major group of Ray Bradbury's invasion stories, those involving the invasion of Mars by Earthmen. Of course, in the tradition of invaders throughout history, when we are doing the invading, it is called "colonization." By having the first Earthmen arrive on Mars in a succession of solitary rockets, Bradbury is able to stage the initial contact of Earthman and Martian several times. Since many of these stories were intended to be read singly, outside the context of a book, the character of the Martians changes to suit the requirements of a particular situation. Thus sometimes the Martians are jealous and brutal, other times they are helpless and complacent. There even seem to be several different intelligent life forms on Mars, each of whom responds to the invaders from Earth in a different way.

The creature in "The One Who Waits," from *The Machineries of Joy*, tells its own story: "I live in a well. I live like smoke in the well. Like vapor in a stone throat . . . I am mist and moonlight and memory . . . I wait in cool silence and there will be a day when I no longer wait." This strange creature has the power, like the giant mushrooms, or the microbes of "Fever Dream" to take possession of other life forms. But this time we experience the story from the creature's point of view.

A rocket lands not far from the well the Martian calls home. Several men approach the well and begin testing the water. The vapor creature allows itself to be inhaled by one of the men:

> Now I know who I am.
>
> My name is Stephen Leonard Jones and I am twenty-five years old and I have just come in a rocket from a planet called Earth and I am standing with my good friends Regent and Shaw by an old well on the planet Mars.
>
> I look down at my golden fingers, tan and strong. I look at my long legs and at my silver uniform and at my friends.
>
> "What's wrong, Jones?" they say.
>
> "Nothing," I say, looking at them. "Nothing at all."

The tables have been turned; the invader has been invaded. One by one, the creature takes over the bodies and minds of the crewmen from the spaceship. It tries each one out as we might try on a new glove. It enjoys the new sensations the men provide it with of touch, taste, smell. It even has one of the crewmen it is possessing shoot himself so that it can temporarily experience death. Like the boy Charles in "Fever Dream," some of the men try to resist the creature:

> I hear . . . a voice calling deep within me, tiny and afraid. And the voice cries, *Let me go, let me go*, and there is a feeling as if something is trying to get free, a pounding of labyrinthine doors, a rushing down dark corridors and up passages, echoing and screaming.

When it finally tires of its game, the creature kills the remaining crewmen by possessing all of them at once and forcing them to throw themselves into the well. The creature then resumes its post, and quietly waits for the centuries to pass.

One reason the first Earthmen are not very successful invaders is that they make no secret about their coming. There is no secret business in Martian cellars, no exploitation of Martian children. The Earthmen swoop down in noisy rocket ships in broad daylight. To make matters worse, the Martians of *The Martian Chronicles* are telepathic, so they can read the Earthmen's minds before a rocket is even sighted. Thus the Martians have plenty of time to prepare a reception. When the first rocket lands in *Chron-*

icles, the crew is simply shot to death by a jealous Martian who fears his wife may fall in love with an Earthman. Another expedition lands on what appears to be the outskirts of a small American town. The crew is welcomed by their own mothers, fathers, relatives, and friends—many long thought to be dead. The Martians have, of course, re-created the town and its inhabitants by reading the crewmen's minds. The crew gradually becomes separated as each member is lured off to what he believes to be his old home. Then, one by one, they are killed.

Actual warfare never does break out between men and Martians. By the time Earthmen arrive in force, most of the Martians have succumbed to diseases from Earth against which they had no immunity. The few Martians remaining abandon their cities and seek refuge in the mountains. The invasion of Mars now goes into full swing. More and more rockets arrive. Lumber and supplies are shipped in, towns are built, and roads are laid connecting them. Benjamin Driscoll, a futuristic Johnny Appleseed, stalks about the planet planting Earth trees. The plains, mountains, and canals of Mars are given new names in honor of rocket pilots, explorers, and remembered places on Earth. The first stage of the invasion is successful: A new population has settled in, and the old population has been driven out. Once the physical invasion has been completed, the more subtle invasion of culture takes place. The Earthmen, like pioneers before them, carry their art, religion, and customs with them. One of the first things an invader does once he has settled on foreign soil is to make his new environment as much like his former home as possible.

In "The Off Season," from *The Martian Chronicles*, the new culture confronts the old. Sam Parkhill opens up a hot dog stand—complete with neon lights and juke box—next to a road he expects will soon be heavily travelled. Parkhill is the personification of the Ugly Earthman: loud, crude, out for the fast buck. One evening a Martian calls on Parkhill. The Martian—a fragile creature, seemingly less substantial than the glass mask and silken robes it wears—has come on a peaceful mission. But the Earthman misunderstands, believing the Martian is attempting to lay claim to the land the hot dog stand occupies. With the arrogance of the conqueror, Parkhill presents the Martian with a few facts of life:

> Look here . . . I'm from New York City. Where I come from there's ten million others just like me. You Martians are a couple dozen left, got no cities, you wander around in the hills, no leaders, no laws, and now you come tell me about this land. Well, the old got to give way to the new. That's the law of give and take. I got a gun here . . .

Before Earthmen completely settle on Mars, nuclear war breaks out on Earth. Most of the Earth people on Mars decide to return to the home planet in its time of need. In a very short time, the Earth settlements on Mars are crumbling ghost towns. Bradbury devotes a number of stories to the fate of the few Earthmen left behind on Mars, or the even smaller number who arrive fleeing the war on Earth. Most interesting are those in which the Earthmen undergo the inevitable metamorphosis and become Martians. The last story in *The Martian Chronicles*, "The Million Year Picnic," treats this theme in a matter-of-fact way. The Thomas family—mother, father, and three sons—learn that the Earth has been all but completely destroyed. They symbolically burn a map of the Earth and, gazing at their reflections in a canal, accept their new identities as Martians.

A more poetic treatment of the metamorphosis theme is found in "Dark They Were, and Golden Eyed," from *A Medicine for Melancholy*. Harry and Cora Bittering and their children Dan, Laura, and David arrive with a number of other families to set up a town on Mars. Harry immediately senses something strange about the atmosphere on Mars. "He felt submerged in a chemical that could dissolve his intellect and burn away his past." Harry expresses his misgivings to his wife: "I feel like a salt crystal in a mountain stream, being washed away. We don't belong here."

The Bitterings and their neighbors build cottages and plant gardens. Each day the rocket from Earth brings the newspaper. Harry reassures himself that all is well: "Why in ten years there'll be a million Earthmen on Mars. Big cities, everything! They said we'd fail. Said the Martians would resent our invasion. But did we find any Martians? Not a living soul! Oh, we found their empty cities, but no one in them. Right?" News of the war on Earth reaches them, and with it the realization that there will be no more rockets for a very long time—that they are in fact trapped on Mars.

Changes slowly begin to occur. The blossoms shaken down from Bittering's peach tree are not peach blossoms. The vegetables from the garden begin to taste subtly different. When Harry visits his friend Sam he begins to notice other things.

> "Sam," Bittering said. "Your eyes—"
> "What about them, Harry?"
> "Didn't they used to be grey?"
> "Well now, I don't remember."
> "They were, weren't they?"
> "Why do you ask, Harry?"
> "Because now they're kind of yellow-colored."
> "Is that so, Harry?" Sam said, casually.

Harry is experiencing a phenomenon common to invaders, that of assimilation. Invasion is not merely an intrusion, unless primarily a military operation. When one culture moves in on another, some sort of mixture will probably occur. All cultures need reinforcement to remain alive. When one population invades another and is then cut off from home, the influence of the host culture strengthens. Harry Bittering is not the first colonial to watch his friends "go native"—but the effect rarely involves a complete transformation into the native species. But this is Mars, and Ray Bradbury's Mars at that. This is a place created by, and subject to, the laws of imagination.

Bittering's family and friends grow taller, their eyes grow more and more golden. Though they've never been taught it, they begin to use Martian words in their conversations. Harry's son Dan declares he is changing his name to Linnl. Laura and David soon become Ttil and Werr. The transformation takes over all of them like some sweet disease. There is no force, no coercion. As they become Martians, they become more relaxed, more at peace with themselves.

Eventually the former Earthmen abandon their town and move up into the Martian hills. The former Bitterings occupy a villa in the Pillan Mountains (formerly the Rockefeller Range, formerly the Pillan Mountains). Months later, Bittering and his wife gaze down at the abandoned Earth settlement in the valley. "Such odd, ridiculous houses the Earth people built," says Harry. His wife answers, "They didn't know any better . . . Such ugly people. I'm glad they've gone."

So the invasion of Mars is over. Bradbury carries his theme of metamorphosis to its ultimate extreme. As in "Fever Dream," and "Boys! Raise Giant Mushrooms . . ." the invader and his victim have become one in the same. Bradbury portrays various life forms—microbe, plant, or human being—moving out from their home worlds to fulfill the need to perpetuate themselves. But he suggests that the price of success might be an ultimate loss of identity. To survive on an alien world, the invader must unite with his victim. Both learn that in order for life to go on, any particular species is expendable, and that the invader's act of aggression may become an act of submission to the higher purpose of life itself.

Bradbury has written only one story in which Martians attempt a military invasion of Earth *à la* H. G. Wells. But the result of the invasion in "The Concrete Mixer" (from the collection *The Illustrated Man*) is quite a bit different from any imagined by Wells. Of course, Wells never saw American pop culture in full flower. Ettil is a peace-loving Martian who only wishes to sit home and read. His fellow Martians are getting ready to invade Earth. Ettil's father-in-law is outraged at Ettil's pacifism: "Who ever heard of a Martian *not* invading? Who!"

Ettil is thrown into prison for draft-dodging. There he is confronted with evidence that he has been reading contraband science fiction magazines from Earth. Ettil readily admits that his sole literary diet has been such fare as *Wonder Stories, Scientific Tales,* and *Fantastic Stories.* He insists that the magazines furnish proof that a Martian invasion of Earth will fail. "The Earthmen know they can't fail. It is in them like blood beating in their veins . . . Their youth of reading just such fiction as this has given them a faith we cannot equal." Ettil is willing to be thrown into a fire along with his beloved magazines rather than join the army, but seeing the disappointment in the eyes of his son, he finally relents.

The Martians are prepared for the worst weapons the Earth might throw at them, but they are quite taken aback by the reception they actually receive. Nurtured on thousands of science fiction stories about invaders from Mars, the Earthmen regard the Martians as superstars. The first rocket to land outside Green Town, is welcomed by the Mayor, by Miss California, a former Miss America, Mr. Biggest Grapefruit in San Fernando Valley, and a brass band playing "California, Here I Come." The rout of the Martian army begins at once. Scarcely have they gotten over being violently ill following helpings of free beer, popcorn, and hot dogs, when they are whisked off to picture shows by amorous women, or pursued by evangelical preachers seeking to save their souls. Ettil is cornered by a Hollywood producer, plied with Manhattans, talked into being technical director for a science fiction film about a wildly improbable Martian invasion. Ettil sinks into a profound depression as he realizes that his fellow Martians are doomed to be lulled by the noisy pleasures of Earth until, one by one, they die in freeway accidents, or of Earth-type afflictions such as cirrhosis of the liver, bad kidneys, high blood pressure, and suicide. Worse, he realizes Earth culture will soon be exported to Mars, and that his quiet home planet will be overwhelmed with night clubs, gambling casinos, and race tracks. One can almost sympathize with poor Ettil when, having stepped into the path of a speeding car being driven by thrill-crazed teenagers, he decides not to get out of the way.

It is not surprising that Ray Bradbury should have written a number of stories about the common science fiction theme of invasion. What is notable is the consistent quality and variety his work exhibits.

Bradbury's stories, like many of his aliens, enter our minds and leave us, perhaps, subtly different from the way we were before.

RAY BRADBURY

Dusk in the Robot Museums: The Rebirth of Imagination

For some ten years now, I have been writing a long narrative poem about a small boy in the near future who runs into an audio-animatronic museum, veers away from the right portico marked *Rome*, passes a door marked *Alexandria*, and enters across a sill where a sign lettered *Greece* points in across a meadow.

The boy runs over the artificial grass and comes upon Plato, Socrates and perhaps Euripides seated at high noon under an olive tree sipping wine and eating bread and honey and speaking truths.

The boy hesitates and then addresses Plato:

"How goes it with the Republic?"

"Sit down, boy," says Plato, "and I'll tell you."

The boy sits. Plato tells. Socrates steps in from time to time. Euripides does a scene from one of his plays.

Along the way, the boy might well ask a question which hovered in all of our minds the past few decades:

"How come the United States, *the* country of Ideas on the March, for so long neglected fantasy and science fiction? Why is it that only during the past thirty years attention is being paid?"

Another question from the boy might well be:

"Who is responsible for the change?"

From *MOSAIC* 13, no. 3–4 (Spring–Summer 1980). © 1980 by the University of Manitoba.

"Who has taught the teachers and the librarians to pull up their socks, sit straight, and take notice?

"Simultaneously, which group in our country has backed off from abstraction and moved art back in the direction of pure illustration?"

Since I am neither dead nor a robot, and Plato-as-audio-animatronic lecturer might not be programmed to respond, let me answer as best I can.

The answer is: the students. The young people. The children.

They have led the revolution in reading and painting.

For the first time in the history of art and teaching, the children have become the teachers. Before our time, knowledge came down from the top of the pyramid to the broad base where the students survived as best they could. The gods spoke and the children listened.

But, lo! gravity reverses itself. The massive pyramid turns like a melting iceberg, until the boys and girls are on top. The base of the pyramid now teaches.

How did it happen? After all, back in the twenties and thirties, there were no science fiction books in the curricula of schools anywhere. There were few in the libraries. Only once or twice a year did a responsible publisher dare to publish one or two books which could be designated as speculative fiction.

If you went into the average library as you motored across America in 1932, 1945, or 1953 you would have found:

No Edgar Rice Burroughs.

No L. Frank Baum and no *Oz*.

In 1958 or 1962 you would have found no Asimov, no Heinlein, no Van Vogt, and, er, no Bradbury.

Here and there, perhaps one book or two by the above. For the rest: a desert.

What were the reasons for this?

Among librarians and teachers there was then, and there still somewhat dimly persists, an idea, a notion, a concept that only Fact should be eaten with your Wheaties. Fantasy? That's for the Fire Birds. Fantasy, even when it takes science-fictional forms, which it often does, is dangerous. It is escapist. It is day-dreaming. It has nothing to do with the world and the world's problems.

So said the snobs who did not know themselves as snobs.

So the shelves lay empty, the books untouched in publishers' bins, the subject untaught.

Comes the Evolution. The survival of that species called Child. The children, dying of starvation, hungry for ideas which lay all about in this fabulous land, locked into machines and architecture, struck out on their own. What did they do?

They walked into classrooms in Waukesha and Peoria and Neepawa and Cheyenne and Moose Jaw and Redwood City and placed a gentle bomb on teacher's desk. Instead of an apple it was Asimov.

"What's that?" the teacher asked, suspiciously.

"Try it. It's good for you," said the students.

"No thanks."

"Try it," said the students. "Read the first page. If you don't like it, stop."

And the clever students turned and went away.

The teachers (and the librarians, later) put off reading, kept the book around the house for a few weeks and then, late one night, tried the first paragraph.

And the bomb exploded.

They not only read the first but the second paragraph, the second and third pages, the fourth and fifth chapters.

"My God!" they cried, almost in unison, "these damned books are *about* something!"

"Good Lord!" they cried, reading a second book, "there are Ideas here!"

"Holy Smoke!" they babbled, on their way through Clarke, heading into Heinlein, emerging from Sturgeon, "these books are—ugly word—relevant!"

"Yes!" shouted the chorus of kids starving in the yard. "Oh, my, yes!"

And the teachers began to teach, and discovered an amazing thing:

Students who had never wanted to read before suddenly were galvanized, pulled up *their* socks, and began to read and quote Ursula Le Guin. Kids who had never read so much as one pirate's obituary in their lives, were suddenly turning pages with their tongues, ravening for more.

Librarians were stunned to find that science-fiction books were not only being borrowed in the tens of thousands, but stolen and never returned!

"Where have we been?" the librarians and the teachers asked each other, as the Prince kissed them awake. "What's *in* these books that makes them as irresistible as Cracker Jack?"

The History of Ideas.

The children wouldn't have said it in so many words. They only sensed it and read it and loved it. The kids sensed, if they could not speak it, that the first science-fiction writers were cavemen who were trying to figure out the first sciences—which were what? How to capture fire. What to do about that lout of a mammoth hanging around outside the cave. How to play dentist to the sabre-tooth tiger and turn him into a house-cat.

Pondering those problems and possible sciences, the first cavemen and women drew science-fiction dreams on the cave walls. Scribbles in soot blue-printing possible strategies. Illustrations of mammoths, tigers, fires: how to solve?? How to turn science-fiction (problem solving) into science-fact (problem solved).

Some few brave ones ran out of the cave to be stomped by the mammoth, toothed by the tiger, scorched by the bestial fire that lived on trees and devoured wood. Some few finally returned to draw on the walls the triumph of the mammoth knocked like a hairy cathedral to earth, the tiger toothless, and the fire tamed and brought within the cave to light their night-mares and warm their souls.

The children sensed, if they could not speak, that the entire history of mankind is problem solving, or science fiction swallowing ideas, digesting them, and excreting formulas for survival. You can't have one without the other. No fantasy, no reality. No studies concerning loss, no gain. No imag-ination, no will. No impossible dreams: No possible solutions.

The children sensed, if they could not say, that fantasy, and its robot child science fiction, is not escape at all, but a circling round of reality to enchant it and make it behave. What is an airplane, after all, but a circling of reality, an approach to gravity which says: look, with my magic machine, I defy you. Gravity be gone. Distance, stand aside. Time, stand still, or reverse, as I finally outrace the sun around the world in, by God! look! plane/jet/rocket—80 minutes!

The children guessed, if they did not whisper it, that all science fiction is an attempt to solve problems by pretending to look the other way.

In another place I have described this literary process as Perseus confronted by Medusa. Gazing at Medusa's image in his bronze shield, pretending to look one way, Perseus reaches back over his shoulder and severs Medusa's head. So science fiction pretends at futures in order to cure sick dogs lying in today's road. Indirection is everything. Metaphor is the medicine.

Children love cataphracts, though do not name them thusly. A cataphract is only a special Persian on a specially bred horse, the combina-tion of which threw back the Roman legions some long while ago. Problem solving. Problem: massive Roman armies on foot. Science fiction dreams: cataphract/man-on-horseback. Romans dispersed. Problem solved. Science fiction becomes scientific fact.

Problem: botulism. Science fiction dreams: to someday produce a container which would preserve food, prevent death. Science-fictional dreamers: Napoleon and his technicians. Dream become fact: the invention of the Tin Can. Outcome: millions alive today who would have otherwise writhed and died.

So, it seems, we are all science-fictional children dreaming ourselves into new ways of survival. We are the reliquaries of all time. Instead of putting saints' bones by in crystal and gold jars, to be touched by the faithful in the following centuries, we put by voices and faces, dreams and impossible dreams on tape, on records, in books, on tv, in films. Man the problem solver is that only because he is the Idea Keeper. Only by finding technological ways to save time, keep time, learn from time, and grow into solutions, have we survived into and through this age toward even better ones. Are we polluted? We can unpollute ourselves. Are we crowded? We can de-mob ourselves. Are we alone? Are we sick? The hospitals of the world are better places since tv came to visit, hold hands, take away half the curse of illness and isolation.

Do we want the stars? We can have them. Can we borrow cups of fire from the sun? We can and must and light the world.

Everywhere we look: problems. Everywhere we further deeply look: solutions. The children of men, the children of time, how can they *not* be fascinated with these challenges? Thus: science fiction and its recent history.

On top of which, as mentioned earlier on, the young people have tossed bombs into your nearest corner art gallery, your downtown art museum.

They have walked through the halls and dozed off at the modern scene as represented by 60-odd years of abstraction super-abstracting itself until it vanished up its own backside. Empty canvases. Empty minds. No concepts. Sometimes no color. No ideas that would interest a performing flea at a dog circus.

"Enough!" cried the children. "Let there be fantasy. Let there be science-fiction light."

Let illustration be reborn.

Let the Pre-Raphaelites re-clone themselves and proliferate!

And it was so.

And because the children of the Space Age, and the sons and daughters of Tolkien wanted their fictional dreams sketched and painted in illustrative terms, the ancient art of story-telling, as acted out by your caveman or your Fra Angelico or your Dante Gabriel Rossetti was re-invented as yet the second giant pyramid turned end for end, and education ran from the base into the apex, and the old order was reversed.

Hence your double Revolution in reading, in teaching Literature and pictorial Art.

Hence, by osmosis, the Industrial Revolution and the Electronic and Space Ages have finally seeped into the blood, bone, marrow, heart, flesh and mind of the young who as teachers teach us what we should have known all along.

Hence this collection of essays which you hold in your hand, regarding and analyzing the phenomenon of the Beautiful Naked Truth walking amongst us unseen. And that Truth again: the History of Ideas, which is all that science fiction ever has been. Ideas birthing themselves into fact, dying, only to reinvent new dreams and ideas to be reborn in yet more fascinating shapes and forms, some of them permanent, all of them promising Survival.

I hope we will not get too serious here, for seriousness is the Red Death if we let it move too freely amongst us. Its freedom is our prison and our defeat and death. A good idea should worry us like a dog. We should not, in turn, worry it into the grave, smother it with intellect, pontificate it into snoozing, kill it with the death of a thousand analytical slices.

This collection should be taken up by all of us who would like to remain childlike and not childish in our 20-20 vision, borrowing such telescopes, rockets, or magic carpets as may be needed to hurry us along to miracles of physics as well as dream.

The Double Revolution continues. And there are more, invisible, revolutions to come. There will always be problems. Thank God for that. And solutions. Thank God for that. And tomorrow mornings in which to seek them. Praise Allah and fill the libraries and art galleries of the world with Martians, elves, goblins, astronauts, and librarians and teachers on Alpha Centauri who are busy telling the kids not to read science fiction or fantasy: "It'll turn your brains to mush!"

And then from the halls of my Museum of Robots, in the long dusk, let Plato have the last word from the midst of his electro-machine-computerized Republic:

"Go, children. Run and read. Read and run. Show and tell. Spin another pyramid on its nose. Turn another world upside-down. Knock the soot off my brain. Repaint the Sistine Chapel inside my skull. Laugh and think. Dream and learn and build."

"Run, boys! Run, girls! Run!"

And with such good advice, the kids will run.

And the Republic will be saved.

WAYNE L. JOHNSON

The Martian Chronicles *and Other Mars Stories*

One evening in Los Angeles in 1949, Ray Bradbury confessed to his friend Norman Corwin his disappointment at not being able to sell a collection of science fiction stories, including stories about Mars, called *The Illustrated Man*. Corwin, a radio and film producer, convinced Bradbury that his best course was to take the stories to New York and seek their publication personally. Bradbury was making little money as a writer at that time, and his wife Marguerite was expecting their first child. Still, the couple managed to scrape enough together to purchase a single round trip Greyhound bus ticket. After four days and nights on the bus, Bradbury checked into a $1.00 a night room at a YMCA in New York, and began visiting publishers. At first the results were discouraging, since there was a limited market for short stories. Then one night in Luchow's Restaurant, Walter Bradbury (no relation), an editor at Doubleday, asked if the Martian stories didn't form some kind of pattern that enabled them to be connected into a novel. Later, back in his room, Bradbury worked up an outline for what was to become *The Martian Chronicles*. The next day, Walter Bradbury not only arranged a contract for the novel, he also agreed to publish the remaining science fiction stories, and these were eventually published as *The Illustrated Man*. Since its original publication in 1950, *The Martian Chronicles* has, as of this writing, gone through more than eighty printings.

From *Ray Bradbury*. © 1980 by Frederick Ungar Publishing Co., Inc.

In his stories about Mars, even those which are not included in *The Chronicles*, Bradbury is consistent. The stories are just as solidly set as those written about Waukegan, Ireland, or Mexico. Of course, unlike these other places, Mars had to be created in effect from thin air. In developing his personal image of what Mars was like, Bradbury drew from both nonfictional and fictional sources. Among the nonfiction sources, the most important are "Mr Lowell . . . and his photographs, and earlier sketches by the Italians of the canals of Mars . . ." Important inspiration from fictional sources came from the writing of Edgar Rice Burroughs and Leigh Brackett.

Of the Italian astronomers, the one who perhaps most influenced the image of Mars as developed by science fiction writers was Giovanni Virginio Schiaparelli. It was Schiaparelli who, in the late 1800s, popularized the term *canali* for the network of fine lines he and other astronomers had observed crisscrossing the planet's surface. Schiaparelli was careful not to suggest that the lines might represent some artificial construction, and in fact *canali* is probably best translated so as to imply a natural channel. Nevertheless, the suggestiveness of the translation "canals" was too great for many people to resist.

The American astronomer Percival Lowell (1855–1916) was deeply impressed by Schiaparelli's drawings and, after observing the Martian canals himself, was convinced that Mars not only supported life, but was home to a race of brilliant engineers. Lowell's studies led him to compose elaborate speculations on Martian geology, climate, and politics. Lowell saw Mars as an ancient world nearing the end of its evolutionary life:

> The drying up of the planet is certain to proceed until its surface can support no life at all. Slowly but surely time will snuff it out. When the last ember is thus extinguished, the planet will roll a dead world through space, its evolutionary career forever ended.

Lowell believed that faced with the evaporation of their oceans into space, and with the concentration of most of the remaining water in the polar ice caps, the Martians undertook an engineering project so huge "the supposed vast enterprises of the earth look small beside it." Noting that "the extreme threads of the world-wide network of canals stand connected with the dark-blue patches at the edge of one or the other of the polar caps," Lowell concluded that the function of the canals was to guide irrigation water to the rest of the planet as one or the other ice cap melted with the change of season. Because of its blood-red hue, Mars has been named after the Roman god of war, and the planet was often associated with its violent namesake. But for Lowell, the planet-wide canal system was evidence of a world at peace with itself: "The first thing that is forced on us in conclusion is the necessarily intelligent and non-bellicose character of the community which could thus act as a unit throughout its globe." Lowell was a respected, if controversial figure, and his theories, as well as the opinions of those debunking his theories, received wide publicity.

As for the fictional influences on his conception of Mars, Bradbury lists Edgar Rice Burroughs as " . . . first and foremost the vulgarian who took me out under the stars in Illinois and pointed up and said, with John Carter, simply: Go There. . . . Without Edgar Rice Burroughs, *The Martian Chronicles* would never have been born."

Burroughs wrote a series of eleven books about Mars, featuring the redoubtable John Carter. Carter, a former officer in the Confederate Army in the Civil War, is mysteriously teleported to the red planet while hiding in a cave from hostile Indians.

Burroughs' Mars is a place of fantasy, with no apologies made. The planet is populated with a bizarre collection of monsters and creatures that resemble human beings, save that they reproduce by laying eggs. Carter goes from one fierce battle to another, pausing occasionally for romantic interludes with scantily clad maidens. Even the surface of the planet, which the inhabitants call Barsoom, resembles a wrestling mat, and is furnished with a "soft and soundless moss, which covers practically the entire surface." The tone of the books is a mixture of Western adventure and sword-and-sandal Biblical epic. The various Martian races are continually at war with one another, and "no male or female Martian is ever voluntarily without a weapon of destruction." The weapons include swords, clubs, and high-powered rifles capable of firing exploding radium projectiles three hundred miles. Martian languages are not very well developed, since most of the population can communicate telepathically. There is a classical touch to Burroughs' Martians too, in that when it is time for them to die, "they go voluntarily upon their last strange pilgrimage down the river Iss, which leads no living Martian knows whither and from whose bosom no Martian has ever returned."

Physically, Burroughs' Mars is similar in many respects to the planet as envisioned by Lowell. The planet is an ancient one, long past its prime. Its seas have evaporated, and the canals are used to circulate water. Burroughs even has the Martians manufacturing their own atmosphere in a special factory. In general, the Burroughs books about Mars are straightforward adventure yarns with an obvious appeal for younger readers. All eleven are still in print, and they continue to be popular in their current paperback editions.

Leigh Brackett, a friend and associate of Bradbury during his early years as a writer in Los Angeles, wrote a number of her own Mars stories. These were obviously influenced by Edgar Rice Burroughs, but boast a refined mythological background and touches of magic and sorcery reminiscent of the writings of the fantasist A. Merritt. Physically, Brackett's Mars is again an ancient planet, crisscrossed with canals and dotted with ruined and half-ruined cities such as "Old Jekkara, with its docks of stone and marble still standing in the dry and dust-choked harbor . . ."

Whatever may be owed to the influences outlined above, Bradbury's Mars is uniquely his own. Like Burroughs and Brackett, Bradbury was not attempting to portray Mars as it actually exists or could exist. But Bradbury was not seeking to write simple adventure stories either. From the start of his project in 1944, Bradbury envisioned an important book about Mars, one which touched upon the deeper human feelings and aspirations. As for the planet itself, Bradbury has never been concerned about the possibility that science would someday prove that there was no life on Mars, or that the planet was quite different from its fictional counterpart. As with Burroughs and Brackett before him, Bradbury's Mars is a mythological place, though in Bradbury's case more classically Greek in atmosphere. *The Martian Chronicles* thus have a certain timelessness about them which even the recent photographs taken from the surface of Mars have failed to dispel. As Bradbury has noted, no one today cares that the Mt. Olympus and the gods of classical Greece never existed. Our encounter with the real mountain does not destroy the power of the myths.

Physically, Bradbury's Mars is a mixture of Lowell's theories and Greek myths. There is a Martian desert which " . . . lay broiling like a prehistoric mud pot," there is a "fossil sea," and canals which "glittered from horizon to horizon." Scattered across the planet are fragile-sounding "ancient bone-chess cities," which contain marble amphitheaters and torch-lit alleyways. In the mountains above the towns are delicate villas with courtyards and fountains. There are roads, but no signs of heavy industry, and only passing references to agriculture.

As with *Dandelion Wine, The Martian Chronicles* is not a novel, but a collection of short stories adapted and linked together by bridge passages. In many cases, the stories which form the *Chronicles* are more varied in tone and less suited to complement each other than are the stories of *Dandelion Wine.* Indeed, some seem quite out of place, being horror tales or fantasies which digress considerably from the main thrust of the book. *The Chronicles* also lacks the unifying effect of a continuous group of characters. A few characters pop up repeatedly through the book, but never to the extent that the book seems to be about them. But it is this very disjointed, episodic structure that gives the book its overall sense of unity, for the *Chronicles* is more than the sum of its parts. The variety of the stories reinforces the feeling that this is indeed a collection of chronicles covering the colonization of a planet. It is something like an elaborate scrapbook in which fact has been bound cheek by jowl with fiction, to give a multifaceted picture of man's relationship with Mars. The book may be roughly divided into three major sections.

The first section deals mostly with the Martians as they prepare for, or deal with, the invasion of Earthmen, and includes the chapters "Rocket Summer" through "The Third Expedition." The three main stories in this section typify the abrupt changes in style and tone which occur throughout the book. "Ylla" is the only real glimpse we get into the daily lives of the Martians before the Earthmen arrive. Mr. and Mrs. K live in a house with crystal walls and fluted pillars. Everything about the house is impressionistically drawn, presenting us with a series of contrasting images. Bradbury combines visual impressions, soft-focused and vague, with tactile images that are sharp and evocative. For instance, we are told that the house turns and follows the sun like a flower, and that the walls are hung with "blue phosphorus portraits"—visual images which tantalize rather than define. On the other hand, the description of the house's cooling system is quite concrete: "A gentle rain sprang from the fluted pillar tops, cooling the scorched air, falling gently on her. On hot days it was like walking in a creek." The cumulative effect of the two kinds of imagery is to produce a mixed impression of both house and occupants which is part real, part dream. Bradbury has us stand with Mrs. K in a house as fragile as a tulip in a garden, while our feet are chilled by water streaming across the floor. This delicate combination of fantasy and reality is one of the major triumphs of Bradbury's Mars.

"Ylla" is also the only look we get at some of the intriguing Martian lifeforms which seem to vanish as the book progresses. The house itself almost seems alive, and there are tantalizing glimpses of flame birds and caged flowers. Martian technology is also hinted at in the lava cooking table, the singing books, and the carpet of fog upon which the Martians sleep. There is even a glimpse into Martian history and "tales of when the sea was red steam on the shore and ancient men had carried clouds of metal insects and electric spiders into battle." And we witness a brief trip on a spectacular mode of transportation, a canopy drawn by mysterious flame birds which flew like ". . . ten thousand firebrands down the wind." Throughout there are touches reminiscent of classical mythology—golden fruits, fluted pillars, wine trees. The story is tied together by the recognizable domestic quarrel which develops between Mr. and Mrs. K. Again, this is our only real look at the interaction of Martians, and their reactions seem surprisingly human.

Bradbury gives us little physical description of his Martians, though brown skin and gold-coin eyes are characteristic traits. Many of the Martians wear masks, which underlines their mystery and the level at which they function as symbols of human dreams about Mars. The ephemeral nature of the Martians and their works contrasts with the more realistically portrayed Earthmen. This functions not only in terms of the plot, but on a deeper level as well. Bradbury was always aware that man might one day reach Mars. Men have dreamt about Mars and other planets for centuries, and science is at last allowing us to confront Mars as it actually is. But scientific data will never be all there is to the Martian experience. The dreams, expectations, and hopes of humankind will go to Mars with every rocket, and our dreams and the scientific information from Mars will interact and color one another. In a way, *The Martian Chronicles* is an extended metaphor for this interaction, and through it, Bradbury is expressing his view of the ways in which dreams and reality coexist in our lives.

"The Summer Night" reinforces the classical Greek atmosphere of Mars, and expands the disturbing telepathic visions which troubled Mrs. K. The tranquillity of the Martian lifestyle, and the unrest the telepathically received thoughts of the Earthmen cause, create a sense of impending doom similar to that faced by the Indians in "Perhaps We Are Going Away."

"The Earth Men" marks quite a jump in tone, a throwback to pulp science fiction. On that level, the story is entertaining, with its satiric view of Martian life, and suggestion that Mars might have its share of what on Earth are UFO fanatics. The conclusion mixes black humor with a touch of the reality-as-function-of-point-of-view theme.

"The Third Expedition" is another improbable tale, but an effective horror story. Mars here provides the sort of fantastic background which allows Bradbury to pull out all the stops and play with themes such as fantasy, nostalgia, magic, illusion, and horror to his heart's content. As is common in such tales, parallels to Bradbury's own art are very close to the surface. In this case, the Martians do to the Earthmen what Bradbury does to us in *Dandelion Wine* and *Something Wicked This Way Comes*, they conjure up an archetypal small town through various sensory images.

"Ylla," "The Summer Night," "The Earth Men," and "The Third Expedition" form a sort of prologue to the *Chronicles*. Their function is not so much to advance the story—which they barely do at all—as to permit Bradbury to recapitulate some of the ways Mars has been treated in fiction: realistically, as fantasy, as pure science fiction, and as the stuff of dreams. The two sections that take place on Earth—"Rocket Summer" and "The Taxpayer"—serve as reference points to which we can return from the more farfetched fantasies. Thus, in this beginning section, Bradbury gets the invasion of Mars off to a good start while avoiding the triteness of a prolonged departure scene. He reminds us of some of the ways Mars has been written about in the past, and tells us that, in the book to come, fact and fantasy will be juggled and juxtaposed.

"—And the Moon Be Still As Bright" begins the main body of the book with an abrupt change in situation. The Martians, who through jealousy or accident or fear destroyed the first expeditions to Earth, have suddenly disappeared. Bradbury again avoids the triteness of an interplanetary war by having the Martians all but exterminated by chicken pox before the chapter begins. This is intriguingly sad, because Bradbury has kept the Martians at arm's length all this time, we've never really had a close look at them, and now, of course, we never will. This chapter introduces the only characters who appear elsewhere in the book, Captain Wilder, Hathaway, and Sam Parkhill. Spender only appears this once, but as one of Bradbury's outsiders, we have seen his like before in William Lantry of "Pillar of Fire," and Montag of *Fahrenheit 451*. It is Spender who does the preliminary research on the Martians, now already the history of a vanished race. Spender discovers a village built of marble with "great friezes of beautiful animals, white-limbed cat things and yellow-limbed sun symbols and statues of bull-like creatures and statues of men and women and huge fine-featured dogs." This suggests that the Martians practiced a sort of Greek pantheism, an idea which Spender finds appealing. We might recall at this point the character George Smith in the story "In a Season of Calm Weather" who encounters Picasso on a beach and watches as the artist draws pictures in the sand: "There on the flat shore were pictures of Grecian lions and Mediterranean goats and maidens with flesh of sand like powdered gold." In any case, Spender finds himself won over to the Martian way of thinking, becoming the first Earthman to turn Martian in the course of the book. But it is Wilder who notes that Martians were ". . . a graceful, beautiful, and philosophical people. They accepted what came to them." If this is true, then Bradbury has given us a hint of what the final days may have been like for the Martians in "The Last Night of the World"—though that story, of course, refers to the last day of Earth. In any case, Spender the idealist, Parkhill the opportunist, and Wilder the pragmatist represent three types likely to be involved in colonization, and their conflict in this early chapter clears the way for the all-out invasion of Earthmen which follows.

The rest of the main section of the book portrays, through vignettes and stories, the settlement of Mars, recalling in many instances the settling of America's West. The stories are, again, a mixture of the plausible and the fantastic. "Way in the Middle of the Air" and "Usher II" do not seem to belong in the context of the other stories, but they function to break up what might otherwise be a pioneer epic and remind us of the social and fantastical elements underlying the book.

The final section of the book begins with "The Luggage Store." Again, the change is abrupt. The colonization seems barely to have gotten started when war breaks out on Earth and most of the colonists return home. Brief attention is given to the fate of those few remaining on Mars, and to the fate of Earth. The book ends with the judgment that humanity's life on Earth represented "a way of life [that] proved itself wrong and strangled itself with its own hands," and with the small consolation that comes from a modest second chance.

Of the themes which run throughout Bradbury's work, the most prominent to appear in *The Martian Chronicles* is that of metamorphosis. Most of the Martians have the ability to change their form to reflect what the Earthmen want to see. In "The Third Expedition" they do this deliberately, but in other chapters, particularly "The Martian," they can be "caught" by a strong Earthman's fantasy and held until a stronger influence comes along or until they can run away. In these cases, the Martians become particularly appropriate metaphors for our dreams. Bradbury seems quite aware that our dreams about Mars are invariably colored by our hopes, and that the reality we eventually confront there will be influenced by both. The Martians' ability to change their appearance is something of a survival mechanism, and it is of course ironic that at the end of the book it is the Earthmen who change into Martians. Thus Mars gives man the chance to change places with his dream, if only in a sad and unexpected way.

Machines play a modest role in most of the book. The machines brought by Earthmen are quite ordinary. The Martian machines reflect a different attitude toward technology, and most are objects of beauty as well as function. Thus the beautiful insect-like walking machine of the Martian in "Night Meeting" contrasts with Gomez's truck. As with the Martians them-selves, most of the Martian machines seem spun from fact and fantasy. Most impressive of them are probably the blue-sailed sand ships described in "The Off Season." Toward the end of the *Chronicles*, however, the machines of men assume a crucial importance. In the back-to-back chapters "The Long Years" and "There Will Come Soft Rains," robots become tragic symbols for man's dreams and hopes gone awry. These stories are probably Bradbury's most successful efforts at making the connection between man's imagination and his machines. In "The Long Years" a man makes robot duplicates of his dead wife and children, robots that continue to live on as a family long after the man himself has died. In "There Will Come Soft Rains" we return for a chilling look at Earth after the atomic war, and witness an automatic house brilliantly yet ignorantly continuing to serve a family long dead. "There Will Come Soft Rains" is Bradbury's favorite story, and both stories are certainly among his most moving. They are effective not only because of the skillfully overlapped ironies, but because they touch upon some of the bewildering craziness of humanity which Bradbury takes a special joy in probing.

Bradbury sees much of man's history as continuing cycles of building, then destroying to build again. It is a pattern we do not seem to be able to break, and those who willingly leave or cannot continue the cycle do not survive. Such is the fate of the Indians of "Perhaps We Are Going Away," and of, say, the ancient Greeks whom the Martians may be seen to reflect. Bradbury's Martians have the good taste to take most of their art and science with them when they die. But Bradbury sees modern man so committed to technology, so given to translating his dreams into machinery, that we may wind up having our dreams survive even if we do not. Recently Bradbury has said: ". . . the dream of mankind has been to someday kill death . . . We . . . cry out to the Reaper: Beware of our rocket, which will shatter your scythe and scatter its bits to the stars." *The Martian Chronicles* expresses, perhaps, the cautious hope that if and when these rockets do reach the stars, they will be piloted by something other than computers.

A number of Bradbury's stories about Mars are not included in the *Chronicles*, though in terms of style and consistency with the stories in the book, they could very well be. In fact, two tales, "The Fire Balloons" and "The Wilderness," not included in the current paperback *Chronicles*, were added to the 1973 hardbound edition. "The One Who Waits" could have been included in the opening section dealing with the first ill-fated expeditions. "The Visitor," which tells of a telepathic young man exiled to Mars is an interesting story, but the main character's power would have weakened the idea of the telepathic capacity of the Martians. "The Strawberry Window" should certainly be read in conjunction with the *Chronicles*, especially as part of the middle section dealing with the lives of the pioneers. "The Exiles," which could be substituted for the chapter "Usher II," finds the spirits of Edgar Allan Poe and other writers seeking refuge on Mars from a sterilized Earth. The story, with its thematic tie-in with "Pillar of Fire" is more obviously a fantasy then "Usher II" but has a more touching, less heavy-handed conclusion than the chapter. "The Messiah" and "The Fire Balloons" both describe encounters between Martians and Catholic priests. The latter story involves a species of Martians not otherwise mentioned by Bradbury, while "The Messiah" has obvious parallels to the chapter "The Martian." "The Other Foot" is a sequel to "Way in the Middle of the Air," though in its implication that blacks are the only Earthmen who settle Mars, it does not fit in with the context of the *Chronicles*. "The Lost City of Mars" and "The Blue Bottle" deal directly with Bradbury's concept of Mars as the repository of man's dreams. Both stories concern groups of people searching for an answer in their lives which the city and the bottle come to symbolize. The power given these objects by the cunning of their creators and by the emotional needs of the searchers reflects, of course, the Bradbury brand of magic. As a result, the successful searchers in both stories encounter not only what they seek, but also, and consistent with the quality of their dreams, what they deserve. "Night Call, Collect" would fit in with the stories of the few men left behind when most Earthpeople return to their war torn home. The story has some interesting parallels with the chapter "The Silent Towns," particularly in the use of the telephones to motivate the main character. In both cases Bradbury has fun with the ambiguous relationships between technology and imagination. The phones in "The Silent Towns" set the main character off in pursuit of a dream girl who turns out to be a very different dream than he had in mind. The phones in "Night Call, Collect" send the main character fleeing from himself and from the frightening results of his warped imagination. Finally, the story "Dark They Were, and Golden-Eyed" is almost an alternate last chapter for the novel, and might be substituted for "The Million-Year Picnic." Both tales involve the metamorphosis of Earthmen into Martians. "Dark They Were, and Golden-Eyed" is the more extended and poetic story, and involves a literal transformation. "The Million-Year Picnic" is more suitable in the context of the book because of the tragic irony in the family's having to become Martians as a matter of survival.

WILLIAM F. TOUPONCE

The Existential Fabulous: A Reading of Ray Bradbury's "The Golden Apples of the Sun"

> *La lecture est du temps perdu si le lecteur n'aime pas séjourner devant les images.*
>
> (Gaston Bachelard)

> A literary text must therefore be conceived in such a way that it will engage the reader's imagination in the task of working things out for himself, for reading is only a pleasure when it is active and creative.
>
> (Wolfgang Iser)

There is no longer any need to situate Ray Bradbury within the larger context of world literature, or to justify a study of his fantasy fiction—perhaps only a need to explain why such a study has not already been undertaken. Gilbert Highet, in his introduction to *The Vintage Bradbury*, places Bradbury's stories in the larger context of the tradition of Western fantasy literature, noting that Bradbury's specific kind of fantasy is not merely supernatural or uncanny: "And beside both horrors and puzzles, he puts beautiful and moving fantasies of a future world where we may be happy as we all wish to be, and memories of a boyhood universe where even the worst monsters

From *MOSAIC* 12, no. 3–4 (Spring–Summer 1980). © 1980 by the University of Manitoba.

can be overcome by energy and confidence." It is this sense of the childhood imagination's transforming power that informs all his work and links him, in the minds of French critics, to the surrealists. Writing in 1965, Highet feels that Bradbury has on the whole been underestimated and misread by American critics, and he predicts that his specific kind of fantasy will win wider recognition in the future.

Can this in any sense be said to have happened? To a large extent, the answer must be negative. Not that Bradbury's texts do not manifest certain effects associated with the genre. They do and they have been observed. But, in this respect, most of the newer critics of science-fiction and fantasy have been preoccupied with finding their own way through the uncharted genealogical jungle, limiting themselves, when not openly hostile, to noting that Bradbury's special preserve is an extreme of elegiac sentiment and gentle fantasy, touched with the eerie and uncanny. What is more, the newer theories of science fiction and fantasy are highly cognitive, stressing the narrative logic of events. To cite two recent examples: for Eric Rabkin, the effect of the fantastic depends on a continuous reversal of narrative ground rules, and he introduces a typology of narrative events to study this effect; for Darko Suvin, science-fiction narration is an operation in cognitive logic which introduces a socio-historical "novum" that estranges the empirical norms of the implied reader, thereby giving a better vantage point from which to comprehend alienated human relations around him. This Marxist critic banishes Bradbury, together with C. S. Lewis, Poe, and H. P. Lovecraft, to the furthest regions of human unfreedom. What is missing in these studies is a sensitivity to the ways in which Bradbury's poetic imagination works, expressed as it is in images that are related to narrative logic only as its transformations. If these critics discuss the Imaginary at all, it is to define it in narrowly generic terms, or to denounce it as a puerile ideological reflex.

Too much emphasis on generic concerns can seriously hamper any insight we might have into the larger significance of a work of fantasy. This problem of external classification seems to have blinded modern fantasy critics who, when they discuss Bradbury at all, ignore his significance as a writer concerned with the human condition. In this regard, Geoffrey Hartman takes what happens at the end of Bradbury's novel of a book-burning state, *Fahrenheit 451*, as a fable for a way out of the problem of modern textual interpretations which in their sophistication have lost the sense of "informing spirit" in a work, and which often simply use a text for their own purposes: "The extinction in this symbolic situation of the personal names of *both* author and reader shows what ideally happens in the act of reading: if there is a sacrifice to the exemplary, it involves the aggrandizement neither of author nor of reader but leads to the recognition that something worthy of perpetuation has occurred." Perhaps, as Hartman suggests, in our society of mass consumption and easy assimilation of literature, that which was meant to convert passive knowledge to active, to bring neglected states of mind to light, becomes subliminal once more. It then becomes the critic's task to defamiliarize literature, to restore it to its full significance as a means to recover the sensation of life which has been deadened by habitual and automatic perceptions. Therefore, in full agreement with Hartman's insights into the reading of Bradbury and in response to the deficiency Highet describes, I present in the following pages an oneiric reading of one of Bradbury's science-fantasy stories, "The Golden Apples of the Sun" (1953).

I have chosen this story because it contains a theme still central to Bradbury's imagination: the romance of space exploration and mankind's quest for identity with the cosmos. "The Golden Apples of the Sun" is a highly mythopoetic text, invoking the myth of Prometheus, among others, in order to suggest a meaning for the mission it describes. The plot involves a handful of men, in a specially-equipped rocketship, whose mission is to bring back to earth a part of the sun which will feed all of humanity with its energy. Yet it offers, I think, irrefutable proof of Bradbury's confidence in reason and progress; for while we are meant to become intimately aware of the functioning of our childhood imagination, we are also led in this way to discover deficiencies in the dominant thought systems and literature of our society. Is there a happier world of childhood reverie dwelling within us, a world of slow and easy time waiting to be awakened? and if so, how is it possible to integrate the feelings of the child, his sense of wonder and novelty at appearances, into the complex intellectual powers of adulthood caught within the existential frame of the human condition? These are questions that Bradbury wrestles with so pertinaciously in this mythopoetic work, questions raised for him by the human drama enacted in contemporary America which was becoming history as he was responding to it. I shall argue that Bradbury's strategy in "The Golden Apples" is to transform then-popular notions of existentialism and Freudian psychology by having the reader explore a certain phenomenological structure of imaginative consciousness, "imaged reverie," whose basic character has been recognized in a series of books on the material imagination by the French philosopher, Gaston Bachelard.

These structures and intentions can be made thematic by a phenomenological theory which affirms that literature is an embodiment of consciousness, and which approaches it through the reading process. Using Bachelard's central ontological category of reverie as a model for a type of literary imagination active in this text, we shall describe it in functional terms as a pattern of communication between text and reader. Respecting the text's temporally-extended nature in reading, we shall allow isolated images produced from the text to stimulate our daydream faculty of mind, reverie, which will in turn prolong and metamorphose these images in a process of anticipation and recollection, and finally link them together in a coherent esthetic response to an imaginary world. This reading method is necessary because it is only by becoming sensitive (while reading) to the existential fabulous which characterizes dreaming that we can properly assess the imaginative *and* cognitive demands of the story—which concern the meaning of existence—and because framed within the narrative is the poetic meaning of why we undertake the journey at all. All of this can be recovered only through reverie, for the story explicitly equates the experience of the mission with a child's grasping of a handful of flowers on a homeward walk from school.

As we shall see, the consciousness that comes to inhabit us as we read this story refers us to Gaston Bachelard's notion of dreaming childhood centered in reposeful object reverie. Bachelard focuses primarily on structures of imaginative consciousness embodied in literature, rather than on the evaluation of a work's specific textual structure as novel, poem or play—a task for which he modestly felt himself to be inadequate since his formal academic training was in the philosophy and history of science. But in all of his literary investigations he was concerned to develop a method of reading imaginative literature (what he termed "oneiric reading" or oneiric criticism) that would not be reductive, that is, one that would give the literary work back its imaginative stature and not reduce it to an aspect of author psychology or of ideology, in the manner of vulgar Marxist and Freudian readings, respectively. As a method of reading, Bachelard's *lire en rêvant* interprets dreams through the dreams we ourselves have in reading the text; thus it restores to us our sense of the autonomy of imaginative productions. In short, Bachelard asserts that works of fantasy have an oneiric logic of invention uniquely their own and quite apart from narrative logic, although related to it.

Object reverie, cosmic reverie *(rêverie cosmique)* based on the four archetypal elements—earth, air, fire and water—and reveries towards childhood *(rêverie vers l'enfance)*, all these structures of consciousness can be found in Bradbury's fantasy, together with their ontological effects: the feeling of well-being with the world, the ecstasy and gentle boredom of the child, the surging of affective memories from childhood, and above all the expansive movement of imaginative consciousness in flights of elated sublimation. The structure of consciousness embodied in "The Golden Apples" is highly complex, and exemplifies, indeed, the most intricate kind that Bachelard discusses in *La Poétique de la rêverie*. The story tends to mingle memory and imagination in an inextricable fashion, and involves a reaching backward in time from the standpoint of adulthood toward object and cosmic reveries we may have had as children, reactivating and reimagining these structures.

Bachelard's felicitous phrase, *rêverie vers l'enfance*, is designed to indicate his special ontology of childhood, so different from the being-towards-death school of the existentialists, and equally different from Freudian analyses of childhood which argue that our imaginative life is to a large extent *determined* by real childhood experiences in the context of the family. Bachelard's ontological inquiry into childhood is concerned with general structures that, as *possibilities*, pervade human existence. In this sense he affirms that a potential childhood is within all of us. When we go looking for it in our reveries, we relive it even more in its very possibilities than in its reality. But Bachelard is quick to remind us that this type of reverie is a definite existential concern, and is not something we can attain from the perspective of adulthood without an openness to the possibilities of childhood. The reverie towards childhood may be blocked by various "culture complexes," as he calls them; beyond parental complexes there are anthropocosmic complexes of Jungian fantasy which, if properly imagined and understood, may provide a counterbalancing response to elements of the dominant thought system which excludes or disparages the phenomenology of astonishment or wonder. Bachelard offers us some suggestions about how the existential fabulous might be accomplished: *"Pour retrouver le langage des fables il faut participer à l'existentialisme du fabuleux, devenir corps et âme un être admiratif, remplacer devant le monde la perception par l'admiration."*

When successful, this type of reverie is marked, according to Bachelard, by a recovery of the language of fables, the original childhood fables that we composed in solitude, for ourselves. It is part of the existential fabulous to take the world given by perception and translate it into a realm of fantasy, as children often do in Bradbury's stories, imagining that some wrinkled old man or woman is indeed a witch from foreign lands. Bradbury has always been sensitive to the ways in which the childhood imagination can irradiate the commonplace with an aura of romance; as existential fabulist, he finds it difficult to accept the social system as something to be explored and described rather than as something to be changed or transcended toward possibilities and freedom (his well-known short story, "The Pedestrian," is a case in point). In Bachelard's ontology of childhood, *angst* or anxiety is not the most general structure in which the world is revealed to us. The child in reverie has not yet taken up the task of confronting non-being; the time of utopian childhood is of the seasons, the very memory of our belonging to the world. Childhood is a being-*for*-the-world, as he playfully remarks.

Formulated in Bachelard's phrase is also an indication of direction, an oneiric direction in which the consciousness of a reader/dreamer returns, following the path opened by the image, to a happier world of mingled memory and imagination outside the responsibilities of the adult world: *"Dans notre rêverie qui imagine en se souvenant, notre passé retourne de la substance."* Further, when we are called towards this region of being, there is a tension set up in consciousness, which we shall interpret as an attempt to detemporalize the narrative process and its concatenation of dramatic events: *"Quand les poètes nous appellent vers cette région, nous connaissons un rêverie tendre, un rêverie hypnotisée par le lointain."* The well-loved image remembered from childhood needs a special, we might even say cumulative or vertical, time to develop. The image gives to words the slow time needed for dreaming, for reverie. Conversely, images are animated in the presence of certain words. One wants to prolong the reverberation of images, to experience and imagine words. This is expressed in a quite lovely manner by "The Golden Apples." For example, when the Captain speaks, the words in his mouth have an imaginary climate and substance: the word "North" dissolves slowly on his tongue like a bit of ice cream. A truly successful reverie towards childhood vanquishes and transforms parental or anthropocosmic complexes opposed to reverie, and becomes a cosmic or world reverie. The dreaming child wants to be at home, in his own special relation to the world. Often this happiness is expressed in oral images. The world is an immense fruit which we eat; there is nothing in it which is alien or harmful to us; we nourish ourselves on the world. We shall explore fully the reverberations of images in this reverie in a moment, but first we need to indicate which structuring elements, as a part of the text's repertoire, will come into play during our reading and produce the poignant tension to which Bachelard refers.

    In the Freudian schema, the development of control over fire and the making of it into the supreme cultural object involves the renunciation of instinctual pleasure and the concomitant development of highly complex ego functions; always there is required a delicate balance of control, a mastery of instinct governing the ability to conserve, confine, extinguish and reilluminate fire. The myths surrounding the acquisition of fire usually indicate that some kind of trick is necessary, and this generates most of the narrative logic of events. In the Freudian schema of civilization and its discontents, the god who is defrauded is the id. Critics of the fantastic such as Rabkin see in the Prometheus myth the story of western civilization's consistently felt fear of the power conferred on it by increasing knowledge. The myth symbolically handles our fears for us. Because Prometheus suffers daily for our sins, Rabkin argues, the sin of our having fire, as well as the guilt for fires gone out of control, belongs to Prometheus, not us. For his part, Bachelard briefly describes the action of the Prometheus complex in *La Psychanalyse du feu* as comprising all the psychic tendencies which drive us to know as much as our fathers, more than our fathers. It designates both the will to intellectuality and the interdictions forbidding it, and it is the "Oedipus complex" of the child's intellectual life. Further, it is only by *handling* the forbidden object (in this case fire, a dangerous one) that we can prove and perfect our knowledge and superiority, rediscovering in the process our primordial relationship to the universe in material imagination. Thus the problem for the child is one of clever disobedience in seizing fire for his own reverie. From this point of view "The Golden Apples" negotiates the prohibitions against playing with fire by a series of negations and dynamic inversions expressed by images of intense heat and cold.

As we shall see, this is the oneiric logic of invention in the story. In order imaginatively to transform the overt narrative level, we must achieve the theft and reappropriation of a pleasure object. When the fire is drawn up into the body of the spaceship, we are able to draw on its power for an imaginative flight of sublimating images which finally allows the resonant image of the child in cosmic reverie to appear in the mind of the Captain. This highly conscious kind of incorporation keeps the reverie substance separate yet accessible to the self as a stable source of pleasure. On the oneiric level, the level of material imagination, the text allows us to participate in the interior life of substance before the interdictions of the Prometheus complex. Thus, as the text shuttles back and forth between the terror and wonder of the Promethean task of scooping out, from the inside of a fantastic supercooled rocketship, a bit of "the flesh of God" (which in a significant passage is referred to as a maternal substance) and the repose offered by images from childhood, we are stimulated to constitute the existential fabulous, the force of imagination under which the events of the text are to be imagined.

This quest story is to be imagined in part under the sign of the child, as how a child might attempt such a journey—hence the fabulous exaggeration we find in certain of its images (packing along two-thousand sour lemonades and a thousand white-capped beers for this journey to the wide Sahara). But our journey through this series of imaginative negations will not be without its price. A certain existentialism of the fabulous will also appear, as death erupts silently on the crew. As a result of blind chance—the structural imperfections of a space suit—one of the crew members is frozen to death. This mechanical failure (one of the possibilities of *things*) is viewed from an adult perspective, as part of the experience of the unreasonableness of the world. This sudden estrangement from a familiar world, in which we feel ourselves as exiles deprived of the memory of a lost home or the hope of a promised land, this divorce between man and his life, was basic to the sensitivity of the absurd widespread in post–World War II existentialist fiction. Of course, we cannot here trace its influences or development in Bradbury's writing, but in "The Golden Apples" itself, Bradbury transforms and intensifies these notions. Working with conventions of the science-fantasy genre, he imagines a voyage through space as an existential situation. There are no signposts to guide us, no North or South, we are faced with absolute annihliation from the sun, and black space threatens to swallow us without a trace. So time and space themselves take on an absolute, forbidding quality

Accompanying the plot is a dialogue between the Captain and his crew which takes the form of questions and answers reminiscent of a small town schoolroom. The text evokes the process of learning authors' names and the titles of their books, in addition to the recitation of poetry. In this manner, the dialogue pre-structures our response to the text by providing us with schemata from which to project images as we search for a solution to the problem that the text poses (the meaning of the mission, in human terms). Naturally, since the narrative, the oneiric and, to a degree, the Freudian fantasy of oral incorporation, suggested perhaps as early as the title—since all of these textual levels interact during the reading process, individual readers will no doubt transform the story somewhat differently. Consequently I have indicated only those passages where the reader's role is to transform fact into the possibilities of oneirism.

We are already in the midst of tension between the narrative and oneiric levels in the opening dialogue. The Captain gives the direction "South" (traveling down towards the sun) and the crew responds in consternation with the scientific answer: "'But,' said his crew, 'there simply *aren't* any directions out here in space.'" This at once gives us a location and a lack of it. Since ordinary space is negated, we must search for something else. The Captain affirms the oneiric direction of the mission, already deep in his own reverie where words have their own climate and dream themselves: "'when you travel on down toward the sun,' replied the Captain, 'and everything gets yellow and warm and lazy, then you're going in one direction only.' He shut his eyes and thought about the smoldering, warm, faraway land, his breath moving gently in his mouth. 'South.' He nodded slowly to himself. 'South.'" In the next paragraph we learn that the ship has several names, at least two of which are mythical: *Copa de Oro* (introducing a flower image which returns later as a synthesizing image of the entire text), *Prometheus* and *Icarus.* These mythical names, as a functional part of the text's repertoire, aid the reader in constructing a reference point for the meaning of the mission. *Icarus* suggests its dangers, *Prometheus* its task, and *Copa de Oro* (cup of gold), the spanish name for a flower, gives us a word-image for reverie which makes poetic the imaginary world that is developing. The game of quotations from literature leaves open paths of reverie into the imaginary worlds of other texts concerned with the problem of the child's relation to the fabulous.

James Stephens' *The Crook of Gold*, for example, is an apocalyptic fantasy in the Irish manner, after Blake. On one level it is an allegory of the human faculties, dislocated in a philosopher's shadowy forest at the outset, but united at the end in a triumphant sunlit return of the dancing pagan gods to Ireland. Caitlin, the central female character who represents mankind's emotional nature, learns that true happiness is to unite the knowledge of man with the gaiety of the child. Stephens exhorts the reader with Blakean rhetoric to come away and quench his heart's desire in a fantasy world where all of the human powers are in balance, (and the leprechauns have their pot of gold to ransom themselves from evil). Steinbeck's historical novel, *Cup of Gold*, the fictional biography of the pirate Henry Morgan, has as its central theme the problem of uniting the child's heart with the man's mind. Young Henry Morgan's dream of becoming a great man and a pirate is symbolized by the Cup of Gold, and he single-mindedly directs all his energies to accomplishing his quest. But when he finally does sack the seemingly inviolable city of Panama (known as The Cup of Gold) with his buccaneers, after a bloody battle in which he kills his best friend, he discovers that his dream has vanished, reduced to a tawdry real cup of gold that he finds in the loot taken from the city. In Steinbeck's novel, Henry Morgan is unable to unite his naive dreams with the civilization he has to face. He sells out his dream and becomes the respected and secure governor of Jamaica. This grounding in literary history aids us in imagining the rainbow trajectory of the reverie by offering us a spectrum of previous solutions to the problem of man's existence and his relationship to a childhood universe. Bradbury uses Yeats and Shakespeare as further climates of the same word. Thus the text evokes history as well as a shared heritage of mythical allusions.

The climates of the text emerge in the following paragraph, with its balancing of frost and fire: "The captain stared from the huge dark-lensed port, and there indeed was the sun, and to go to that sun and touch it and steal part of it forever was his quiet and single idea. In this ship were combined the coolly delicate and the coldly practical. Through the corridors of ice and milk-frost, ammoniated winter and storming snowflakes blew. Any spark from that vast hearth burning out there beyond the callous hull of this ship, any small firebreath that might seep through would find winter slumbering here like all the coldest hours of February." From this passage, which poeticizes sensation and substance, oneiric criticism can discern the emergence of the Prometheus complex: "to go to that sun and touch it and steal part of it forever was his quiet and single idea." In this story, in order to inhabit the dream of touching the sun, the child first cleverly renounces fire, inhabits corridors of frost. He imagines a pure climate of childhood, a condensation of all the coldest hours of February. February is absolute, yet humanized cold, a season that protects the dreamer from the "spark" or germ of any other reverie that might interfere with his quiet and single idea. In the scientific view of thermodynamics we know, of course, that cold is merely the absence of heat. The "realistic" means for attaining our goal is imaged as a spaceship which embodies the sterile purity of technology. But the narrative and oneiric levels interpenetrate. Ammoniated winter slumbers in repose and would contain any warming breath that tried to melt it. Following the dynamism of the oneiric images, we learn that cold is a force in itself, and that it becomes cold by expelling heat. This is further complicated and complemented by the fact that inside the super-cold world of the rocket the men are protected by insulating suits (which protect the poet's warming breath), another variation on the dream of dynamic containment prominent in the story. This is one example of a logic that is not so much narrative or cognitive as it is poetic, a kind of oneiric logic of invention that parallels events in the story—which is why Bradbury frames the statement of his character's Prometheus complex within the coolly delicate and the coldly practical.

Of course, the narrative direction of the story is toward the "real" sun, and the Captain and crew are in danger of being destroyed. A surrealistic thermometer keeps speaking the temperature in degrees Fahrenheit, as if it could feel the pressure of the two climates and the approach of the oneiric source. It murmurs the fantastic and fearful temperatures in the arctic silence of the ship, as it touches the sun. These interjections are a measure of desire, and a compass for the poetic action of the story. In the following passage, an element from the narrative level of the text is juxtaposed with the instantaneous moment of the image which opens the path to reverie again: "'Now we are touching the sun.' Their eyes, thinking it, were melted gold." In order to bridge this reading gap between fact and imaginative consciousness, the dreamer and the image, subject and world, must be interrelated on the same level of being. The collective vision of the captain and crew is melted into a substance which expresses the admiring being of them all. Gold is at once their admiration and their pride at seeing the big and beautiful sun, and the reciprocal look between them and the world. Through this image, we gain access to the realm of the fabulous, a land of conquest and plunder beyond the rainbow. If we dwelt long with this image, we would find our reverie which loosens the thread of narrative. But Bradbury quickly puts us into another absolute climate of childhood, "'Four thousand degrees Fahrenheit!' Noon. Summer. July."

At this moment, the text introduces a question and formulates an answer: "'What *time* is it?' asked someone. Everyone had to smile. For now there was only the sun and the sun and the sun and the sun. It was every horizon, it was every direction. It burned the minutes, the seconds, the hourglasses, the clocks; it burned all time and eternity away. It burned the eyelids and the serum of the dark world behind the lids, the retina, the hidden brain; and it burned sleep and the sweet memories of sleep and cool nightfall." The violence of this passage, which seems to destroy the duration of reverie and any reference point that might help us, brings to the fore another aspect of Bradbury's existentialism of the fabulous. The dreamer cannot live in this absolute climate. The sun has burnt out "the hidden brain," the "serum of the dark world behind the lids," anywhere, in short, that consciousness could find repose in a beautiful image. The fulfillment of reverie and desire, the touching of the sun, will bring death into the crew, and the ship will begin to melt.

Paradoxically, however, although one man will be killed for breaking the interdiction, it will be from cold. Because of a "structural imperfection," Bretton, the first mate, is frozen to death in his suit. The image of death's substance is a kind of frozen milk, a maternal substance which no longer nourishes us: "Inside Bretton's plastic face-mask, milk crystals had already gathered in blind patterns. They bent to see." The blind pattern of Bretton's death will be compensated for later, however, by an "unborn child," a child of fire drawn up into the body of the ship. The flesh of the sun, which the huge mechanical hand is about to touch, "set out and mothered a galaxy" long ago. Here we find expressed a fantasy of incorporation or union with the mother; but perhaps it is not so much the desire to lose the self as to be reborn again, for reverie must be centered on an object, present to itself, and conscious. Bradbury directs us to a region of reimagined childhood memories, pure memories which have no history, but only a season: "As if a motion picture projector had jammed a single clear memory frame in his head, he found his mind focused ridiculously on a scene whipped out of childhood. Spring mornings as a boy he found he had leaned from his bedroom window into the snow-smelling air to see the sun sparkle the last icicle of winter. A dripping of white wine, the blood of cool but warming April fell from that clear crystal blade. Minute by minute, December's weapon grew less dangerous. And then at last the icicle fell with the sound of a single chime to the graveled walk below."

This experience of finding one's mind ridiculously focused on a scene is reminiscent of Camus's famous description of the Absurd: the gestures of a man talking on the telephone behind a glass partition suddenly become mechanical, a meaningless pantomime, and slowly the feeling of absurdity spreads to the world. But the "clear memory frame" whipped out of childhood is not, strictly speaking, a memory at all. It is the awakening consciousness of childhood reimagined and remembered in terms of its reverie. At first glance, this memory might seem completely kinetic and mechanical. Men, too, secrete the mechanical, as we may remember from Camus. The picture seems cinematic (to follow the simile) and external to the consciousness which sees it. But if we examine the direct images of matter in this text, we are drawn into the glimmers and limbo of an intimate crossing of boundaries between the two climates. The boy finds himself leaning out from within an enclosed space to discover the world and his own consciousness of it at the same time. Here we can observe a natural myth forming around the combat of the seasons, expressed in "December's weapon" and "April's blood." Both climates of the story in fact block a happy reverie. The ice and snow of winter possess an absolute exteriority, the pure apparition of a hostile non-self. Nor could a dreamer interiorize the annihilating sun. But with the mixing of the seasons in Spring, a dynamic inversion takes place in the interior of substance. Active inside the cold, slumbering in repose, is heat. Both white wine and the blood of cool but warming April are interior substances becoming less and less dangerous for a dreamer. This is a reverie of substance, of the repeated, durational time of many Spring mornings. The seasons of childhood, which were in such conflict with each other, are mixing. There is a wounding, a sense of existence trying itself out in a world increasingly commanded by the sun. But the child's consciousness has not yet taken upon itself the task of confronting non-being. The deliquescence of the icicle is the *matter* of this ontological condition which has nuances of both being and non-being. So the clear memory frame is a photograph, esthetically composed, but reverie has provided the time and light for the picture to be ample. It has given duration and beauty to this image confided to memory.

In this manner, in the astonishment of the moment, the Captain is drawn out of the forward movement of events occurring in the ship toward the memory of an old childhood reverie. This image of the melting icicle, which is also the ship itself, again grounds us in the imaginative experience of matter and tries to draw us, and the Captain, into the solitude and security of a cosmic reverie where we would rediscover the language of fables. The Captain is indeed "hypnotized by a far away region." The references to "December's weapon" and "crystal blade" suggest a mythical world of childhood fantasy. He has entered, if only briefly, into the different ontological time of reverie. This detemporalization of the narrative process cannot, of course, stop the "film" from running for long. As the ship loses more refrigeration, the Captain is assailed by images of the future: he and his crew are ants in a flaming matchbox, space would drown out their screams like a black-mossed well. Needless to say, these images, one of being burnt up in a kind of superconsciousness and the other of falling into unconsciousness, are too strong for the dreaming child. Although they do represent the existential anxiety of complete annihilation in space, because of how frightening they are we cannot enter into them for long: "we're used to more leisurely dyings, measured in minutes and hours."

The next narrative sequence involves the operation of the gigantic metal hand which holds the Cup. The Captain operates it from within a robot glove. This highly coordinated task is a product of the developed rationality of consciousness and technology, but we should remember that for the Prometheus complex the crucial moment is the handling of one's own fire. There is already an oneiric movement in the way this fantastic gigantic hand magnifies the slightest twitch of the Captain's hand, providing a "tremendous image of his own gesture." The text gives us the imaginary double of the hand, immediately translating us to the oneiric level of the text, offering instantaneous fulfillment of desire. Above all, we should note that it is a *beautiful* hand which, once it has stolen the gift of fire, drips yellow flowers and white stars. In this dream of the hand touching the body and flesh of creative matter, of stealing solar light and a bit of divine intelligence, the Prometheus complex is transformed, sublimated. The sterile purity and economy of technology have captured a beautiful excess. The archetypal image of the human heart and its desires, the Cup, now contains the gift that "might burn forever." If as Bachelard suggests, the Prometheus complex is the Oedipus complex of intellectual life, then the wish to be the father of one's own reverie is here fulfilled. The sun's flesh is the ultimate matter, the golden fruit of the world of the imagination. Bradbury invites all of humanity to participate: "And here is our cup of energy, fire, vibration, call it what you will, that may well power our cities and sail our ships and light our libraries and tan our children and bake our daily breads and simmer the knowledge of our universe for us for a thousand years until it is well done. Here, from this cup, all good men of science and religion: drink! Warm yourselves against the night of ignorance, the long snows of superstition, and the cold winds of disbelief, and from the great fear of darkness in each man."

In this passage, a kind of ultimate cultural sublimation has taken place. There is no indication that the sun's secret will destroy us; instead, the Prometheus complex has been destroyed! No longer will it block the path to reverie. Even when the Captain comes to equate his act with that of a caveman discovering fire a million years ago on a lonely northern trail—in a passage that is more the representation of scientific ideology than reverie— the caveman finds a kind of sensuous enjoyment in the gift of "summer" before the interdiction of the Prometheus complex. In Bradbury's text at least, the advent of culture does not prevent the beginning of reverie. For the dreaming child, culture would be the extension of a natural reverie. As the Captain thinks of the new season in their cave, he offers us an image of the fire, that newly acquired object, that is almost a flower, "this small yellow spot of changing weather."

Cooling, its heart pulse slowing, the ship turns away from the fire of the sun, while "the thermometer voice chanted the change of the seasons." If we have followed the oneiric level closely we might expect the text to break into poetry, to compose with images that sing reality, because reverie wants to use language as praise. As the crew thinks with mild insouciance about the ultimate dream of controlling the climates of the imagination ("they might even dismantle some refridgerators, let winter die"), the Captain, tending now to Bretton's body, remembers a poem he had composed many years before. The crew is living through a dynamic inversion of major proportions. Normally, we speak of "letting the *fire* die," and the price of our mastery over fire is never letting it go out. It involves us in a vigilance that requires the renunciation of instinct. Now it is possible to let winter's slumbering power die. What an inversion of the renunciation of instinct, won through reverie! The Captain's poem celebrates and commemorates the new reality, pinpointing the general significance of the events in the story:

> Sometimes I see the sun a burning Tree
> Its golden fruit swung bright in airless air
> Its apples wormed with man and gravity
> Their worship breathing from them everywhere,
> As man sees Sun as burning Tree. . . .

The golden fruit that the Captain celebrates is the beauty of the new world, now that they have the sun within them. There are many echoes in this poem, which mingles lyric religiosity and humanism. Centering the poem is the archetype of the cosmic tree, bearing the World Fruits which solicit our reverie and invite our happiness. There are suggestions of lost paradise, the burning bush from which God speaks to Moses, the classical myth of the Hesperides, the blessed isles, and, of course, Yeats's famous poem about the wandering Aengus. Yet there is a hint of elegiac sadness, a paradox linking us to the world, for Bradbury finds the golden apples "wormed with man and gravity." Gravity is, after all, what holds the human spirit down. It is gravity which causes the icicle to fall from the rooftop, breaking the child's reverie. We know that the sun breathes in airless air; perhaps, as the existentialists affirm, it is only in resolutely facing up to the encounter with death and nothingness that we become automatically human. At the heart of the golden apple of being, nothingness lies coiled like a worm. Nevertheless, there is still the human possibility of seeing the world sometimes transformed by the child's fabulous imagination.

The boy with a handful of dandelions is perhaps the most poignant image of the story, a harmonic or vertical moment uniting the past, present and future: "The captain sat for a long while by the body, feeling many separate things. I feel sad, he thought, and I feel good, and I feel like a boy coming home from school with a handful of dandelions." The Captain, and we as readers, takes the path of the image again, towards a reverie of childhood. The image is poignant because in it the Captain discovers the true source and value of what he has accomplished, despite its cost. The Promethean task, the cosmic gesture of stealing the energy of the sun for the benefit of humanity, has awakened the wonder of potential childhood within us. On the oneiric level, the text searches for a childhood without complexes, lives through a series of inversions and negations. We learn that the child too has his cosmos, the image. If there are scientific truths, then there are also oneiric truths. Even as we cross the summer fields of childhood, we are crossing the cosmos.

Bradbury structures a great deal of reverberation into this image. We find that it echoes variationally through the text at crucial oneiric moments—Copa de Oro, the oneiric goal of the text, which drips yellow flowers, the cultural taming of fire which presents us with the small yellow spot of changing weather. This image of repose, of tranquility and comfort, of basking in the illumination of the sun's own flowers, liberates us from the responsibilities of the adult world. The Captain is finally at rest, having accomplished his dream. The little boy who has escaped from the schoolroom where culture complexes are learned and grafted onto an increasingly forbidden childhood already has stolen the fire of the sun. In dreaming on these flowers, the Captain must have dreamt his mission long before accomplishing it.

The image of the handful of flowers recapitulates the success of the mission, but it would be a mistake to think that images in this story simply echo the past. Because they are open and communicable acts of consciousness addressed to a permanent core of childhood within us, their direction is also towards the future direction, home: "'When you've gone a long, long way down to the sun and touched it and lingered and jumped around and streaked away from it, where do you go then?'" The crew does not respond, as it did at the beginning of the story, with a scientific answer. Its consciousness, together with ours as readers, has changed during the cosmic encounter. There is no problem with the communicability of the reverie; we have all experienced the same reverie: "His men waited for him to say it out. They waited for him to gather all of the coolness and the whiteness and the welcome and refreshing climate of the word in his mind, and they saw him settle the word, like a bit of ice cream, in his mouth, rolling it gently." This image of cold in the mouth dynamically balances the image of hotness contained in the ship. It is an image of cold within warm, of the word's changing climate in the poet's warming breath. No longer is winter "ammoniated," but now it can be eaten without any care at all. In the original joys of childhood, says Bachelard, the world is edible. "'North,' murmured the captain. 'North.' And they all smiled, as if a wind had come up suddenly in the middle of a hot afternoon." The word "North" is spoken within a collective reverie of the Captain, crew and us as readers. It brings the special climate of childhood where words dream. Have we not felt the poet's element by which the words of reverie live and breathe throughout this story? is it not within a cool but warming climate that the Captain speaks his poem about the golden apples of the sun, "their worship breathing from them everywhere," both North and South?

Bradbury has given us a fable of modern consciousness which often forgets, in its urge towards progress and technology, its Promethean debt to the unconsciousness. In the long story of mankind's quest for knowledge, he has transformed Prometheus into a child dreaming close to oneiric sources. Yet it should be clear, from the temporal and historical perspectives that open up even in this highly mythopoetic text, that he is not a writer who seeks solely to dissolve consciousness in some archaic mystical fog, as some critics doubtless believe. The nature of what Bradbury was after in his fantasy will probably continue to be overlooked if the assessment of his stories remains at the level explored by the emotive-cognitive distinction. I hope that I have made some useful suggestions as to how Bradbury might profitably be read in the future.

HAZEL PIERCE

Ray Bradbury and the Gothic Tradition

Anyone seeking to connect a contemporary author with any established literary tradition must heed Coleridge's prefatory remarks to "Christabel" in 1798. To protect himself from charges of "servile imitation," Coleridge came right to the point:

> For there is amongst us a set of critics, who seem to hold that every possible thought or image is traditional; who have no notion that there are such things as fountains in the world, small as well as great; and who would therefore charitably derive every rill they behold flowing, from a perforation made in some other man's tank.

Coleridge did admit an alternative when in "Kubla Khan" he described a fountain which "flung up momently the sacred river," creating a tumult in which could be heard voices. After tapping the ancient source and tossing its elements into new life, the fountain returns them, energized, to enrich the original flow.

Similarly, an author can tap a literary tradition and, in playing his own variations on its themes and conventions, leave it richer for the diversion. In an interview in 1976, Ray Bradbury faced a question that touches close to

From *Ray Bradbury.* © 1980 by Martin Harry Greenberg and Joseph D. Olander.

that of Coleridge: are authors inventors of ideas or trappers of independent sources? Bradbury rejected both the idea of invention and that of borrowing. For him, the author's purpose is to find fresh ways of presenting basic truths. In the interview Bradbury did not discuss the forms in which writers might embody these fresh insights; but close reading of certain short stories and novels reveals that he has not rejected traditional modes when they fit his purposes. Three volumes merit attention: *The October Country* (1955), a collection of short stories; *Something Wicked This Way Comes* (1962); and *The Halloween Tree* (1972). In these stories and novels we find Bradbury's use of the conventions, themes, and mood of the Gothic tradition, as well as the changes he has made, thus giving it fresh energy and new range.

Proto-gothic tales of mystery, such as ghost stories, fairy tales, and adventures into dark unknown reaches of a nether world, are found in the folklore of most cultures. The Gothic tradition cannot boast of a long nor always honored literary presence. For many years, the very term *Gothic* bore the pejorative connotation of *barbarous*. Reassessment of this view became necessary as critics found respected writers using certain "Gothic" elements. Writing his *Letters on Chivalry and Romance* in 1762, Bishop Richard Hurd speculated on Gothic touches in such poets as Spenser and Milton, asking: ". . . may there not be something in the Gothic Romance peculiarly suited to the views of genius, and to the ends of poetry?" Nonetheless, when publishing *The Castle of Otranto: A Gothic Story* in 1764, Horace Walpole felt the need to hide behind the persona of a translator. He affixed his own identity to the second edition only after he was assured of a happy reception for the book.

Almost a century later, in 1854, John Ruskin devoted a chapter of *The Stones of Venice* to Gothic architecture. He acknowledged that all people "have some notion, most of us a very determined one, of the meaning of the term Gothic." At the same time, he requested understanding from any reader who might think that he was interfering with "previously formed conceptions" or was using the word in any sense which the reader "could not willingly attach to it." Particularly, Ruskin directed their forbearance and consideration to his six "moral elements" of the Gothic style: Savageness, Changefulness, Naturalism, Grotesqueness, Rigidity, and Redundancy. Of course, he was writing about architecture, not literature. But his ideas did receive consideration and influenced not only the Victorian view of Gothic architecture but its literary aesthetics as well.

Anyone writing of gothicism in the novel today faces one of the problems Ruskin faced—"previously formed conceptions." One anticipates the question: "Which Gothic?" Since Walpole's novel of 1764 initiated a literary vogue, the mode has alternated between the heights of popularity and the depths of critical disapproval. During the waves of popularity, its practitioners added machinery, shifted the thematic emphasis, and experimented with unique combinations. Today we are at the point where there are several models, all of which can be called *Gothic*. Despite their surface differences, all of them share a common forefather and a core of common conventions.

In the preface to the second edition of *Otranto*, Walpole explains his intention to "blend the two kinds of Romance, the ancient and the modern." Ancient Romance would add "imagination and improbability" to the modern which, in turn, would copy nature by a "strict adherence to common life." To these ends Walpole described realistic settings, despite the fact that they smacked of an earlier medieval period. One expects a castle to have "intricate cloysters" with heavy doors and secret vaults fitfully lit by torches. One also expects these castles to be inhabited by people of rank who most probably would hang paintings of their illustrious forebears on the dimly lit walls of the "Great Hall."

The ancient Romance added creaking hinges to the heavy doors, fitful drafts to blow the torches out at opportune times, and hollow groans and sighs echoing through the galleries. Walpole fitted a trapdoor into one room of his "subterraneous regions," thus allowing access to still deeper caverns leading to sanctuary in a church. The moon of ancient Romance usually gleams pallidly, lighting nefarious activities while claps of thunder shake castles to their very solid foundations at the moment when apparitions stalk the staircases. In Walpole's novel the ancient Romance proved the more dominant, for a general atmosphere of mystery and wonder pervades this early novel.

Paradoxically, *Otranto* enjoyed its greatest popularity in the last half of the eighteenth century, that period noted for elevating reason over emotion and the mind over the senses. As one would expect, the novel spawned numerous imitations. Fortunately, it also stimulated two authors to expand the model with rewarding success: Mrs. Anne Radcliffe (*The Mysteries of Udolpho*, 1794, and others) and Matthew Gregory Lewis (*The Monk*, 1796). Between them, they divided the river of Gothic writing into two distinct streams. By adding a strain of sentiment to her plots, Mrs. Radcliffe refined mystery and wonder into terror; "Monk" Lewis eliminated sentiment and sympathy, thereby pushing past terror into the depths of horror.

In Mrs. Radcliffe's novels, sentiment encourages degrees of sympathy for her virtuous female victims, a response which Walpole's Isabella never elicits from a reader. She expands the threatening settings. Her Udolpho, a "vast, ancient and dreary" structure of "gothic greatness" with "mouldering walls of dark grey stone" stands "silent, lonely and sublime" but "frowning defiance at intruders." Even the natural environment is inhospitable. At one point in *Udolpho*, Emily must escape the villainous Montoni by traveling down gloomy paths, through immense pine forests, past lofty crags and falling cataracts. As expected, a pallid moon lights her path. Gothic characters operate in a perpetual man-made or natural setting of "gloomy grandeur or of dreadful sublimity." In the end, youth and love win out, defeating tyranny and restoring proper authority, and all irrational happenings receive rational explanations to calm the reader.

"Monk" Lewis defied this need to return to the rational world. In his novel, decadence replaces dreadful sublimity, while eroticism replaces sentiment. *The Monk* shifts setting from castle to abbey, with a concomitant shift from cruel nobleman to corrupt monk. The shift is only surface, for both worlds represent corrupted authority. In Lewis's novel the monk, Ambrosio, rapes a drugged and helpless Antonia in the gloomy catacombs. Later, in an equally gloomy dungeon of the Inquisition, Ambrosio summons up Lucifer to strike a bargain. From beginning to end of *The Monk*, the author compounds one horror with another, culminating in Ambrosio's death on "the seventh day" when a mighty storm finishes what bruising rocks, eagles ripping at flesh, and raging thirst have not already accomplished. The novel abounds in events that defy rational explanation and which provoke moral revulsion.

Inevitably, satiation set in. The vogue for the Gothic story began to wane during the first decades of the nineteenth century. Jane Austen, for one, satirized it in *Northanger Abbey* (1818). But the tradition did not die; it went underground temporarily, like Coleridge's sacred river "through caverns measureless to man," finding in the Victorian years other fountains to fling it up. In the second half of the nineteenth century the sensational story became popular with such practitioners as Charles Dickens, Wilkie Collins, Joseph Sheridan Le Fanu, Bulwer-Lytton, Robert Louis Stevenson, and Oscar Wilde. The country house, the vicarage, even the fashionable town house replaced the medieval castle and abbey in many tales of sensation. Mystery and wonder operate on a lonely Wuthering Heights as well as in a castle of Udolpho or Otranto. Personal guilt and fear of a threat from the present, rather than from the past, marked this resurgence of the Gothic mode.

On the other side of the Atlantic the tradition took new paths in the work of Charles Brockden Brown, Nathaniel Hawthorne, Edgar Allan Poe, and others. American authors recognized the new opportunity which a fresh environment had offered them. For example, Brown rejected what he called "puerile superstition and exploded manners, Gothic castles and chimeras." In "To the Public," his prefatory statement to *Edgar Huntly* (1799), he early staked out a claim for the American novelists in stating that "the incidents of Indian hostility, and the perils of the Western wilderness, are far more suitable." Despite this pronouncement, John Keats, in a letter to his friend Richard Woodhouse, in 1819 referred to the genius and "accomplished horrors" of Brown's *Wieland*, referring to Brown himself as "a strange american scion of the German trunk." In the preface to *Tales of the Grotesque and Arabesque*, Poe defended himself against a similar charge of Germanism, which he called "that species of pseudo-horror."

Poe is a major link between Ray Bradbury and the Gothic tradition. In the interview referred to above, Bradbury gives ample credit to the short stories of Poe for helping create that "fantastic mulch" in his head from which he can recall what he needs at any time. What special contribution could Poe have made? Certainly he offered an introduction to at least one of the older Gothic writers. In "The Oval Portrait" Poe describes a chateau as "one of those piles of commingled gloom and grandeur which have so long frowned among the Apennines, not less in fact than in the fancy of Mrs. Radcliffe." In "Thou Art the Man" Poe speaks of all "the crack novels of Bulwer and Dickens." Again and again, he drops names, mentioning metaphysical thinkers, writers of German romances, experimenters, and occultists of his time.

Painters associated with the Gothic vogue found their way into Poe's work. A prime example is John Fuseli, an eccentric friend of William Blake, painter-fantasist of man's nightmare's. His psychopathological representations, as we might call them today, touched a kindred sensitivity in Poe. When Poe mentioned Fuseli in "The Fall of the House of Usher," did the name lie quietly in Bradbury's mind until he drew it out to use in his own story, "Skeleton"?

In his reading of Poe, the youthful Bradbury could not have overlooked the awareness of what makes the hair on the back of the neck stand on end. What happens to reason when its ordered reality undergoes fission or fusion? These words with reference to Poe have to do with psychic or spiritual energy, not nuclear energy. Actually, Poe's own terms serve better—the terms *grotesque* and *arabesque* in his *Tales of the Grotesque and Arabesque*.

While Poe denied that his tales smacked of Germanism, that "pseudo-horror," he did admit that they presented "the terror of the soul," but only as derived from legitimate sources, and leading to legitimate results. In these claims he offers his own brand of Walpole's blend of ancient and modern Romance. In those tales best described as grotesque, the reality of common life is distorted or destroyed when time, space, or self is abnormally affected. In the tales of the arabesque, workaday reality shimmers, flows, and fuses into strange and beautifully terrible forms. Here in this new reality, time, space, and self exist as an uncommon unity. The departure from the norm elicits fear in the heart and mind of a rational being.

The Gothic tradition is based firmly on the very human emotion of fear. Its tales plumb the fear of death and the unknown, of the unexplainable and unknowable. Occasionally the fear is pleasurable pain, born of sheer astonishment and bringing vicarious thrills. At the other extreme, the vividness of the terror or horror of the human situation turns the reading of a Gothic tale into a nightmare. An author who can subtly dissect human weakness and motivation and then expose them to irrational manipulation may well touch a reader's exposed nerves with the energy of fear.

Hand in hand with the fear of the unknown is the well-known, age-old fear of evil. Gothicism, which is concerned with the struggle with evil, balances the fear with a strong strain of idealism and optimism. Underlying the mystery and suspense runs the tenuous hope that when the light of the sun dispels the dark shadows, good will eventually win out over evil. Even here, though, reason must contravene with the full knowledge that good and evil, light and dark, in defining each other are committed to eternal coexistence.

In the first half of this century a growing interest in realism and naturalism worked against Gothic writing. Now, in the latter half of the century, it is gradually reasserting itself. What Irving Malin calls *New American Gothic* is evident in many mainstream novels where the "subterraneous regions" lie in the darkness of the individual psyche, and where the fear roots itself in individual guilt, an inability to love, or withdrawal from the larger society. Like Poe, modern authors probe man psychologically but with the benefit of decades of behavioral studies to draw on.

In this century, a mass-audience Gothic novel closely identified with the Walpole-Radcliffe-Lewis triad is enjoying a resurgence of popularity. Witness the use of "Gothic Romance" as a trade label, for example. Many of these popular romances are derivative to the point that the old machinery has degenerated into pure claptrap and trumpery, as its severest critics maintain. Medieval settings have returned to share use with large Victorian-style mansions, for today's persecuted heroine has the airplane to fly her to such locations. Charles Brockden Brown's perils of the Western wilderness have resurfaced as perils of the patrolled camping site or the after-hours warehouse wilderness. Modern satanic cults, international terrorists, and Mob-like organizations easily do the work of the early robber bands and the Illuminati, that secret society so beloved of early romancers. In our world modern Frankensteins bend over technological "monsters" which threaten to elude their control. Secret manuscripts translate into secret code books to aid undercover spies.

Some items of the old Gothic machinery need no modern counterparts; they are the ones that shape our night dreams. Strange noises, spectral manifestations, abnormal personality changes—all have weathered the decades well. Today the entire package is still wrapped in gloom, darkness, thunder, lightening (effects especially well managed by the film-makers). Most of these popular novels are, in Coleridge's words, "rills flowing from a perforation made in some other man's tank," possibly that of Walpole, Mary Shelley, or Edgar Allan Poe. Such "servile imitation" indicates either a contempt for or mistrust of the power of the human imagination.

The author with faith in his own imagination can put that old machinery and its modern additions to good use. We might rephrase Bishop Hurd's original query, "may there not be something in the Gothic Romance peculiarly suited to [illuminating modern man's dilemma, especially if handled by a poet]?" Devoted readers of Bradbury have long recognized him as a poet in the fullest sense of the word—a maker and doer with words. Out of his story of memory he can summon a theme, a convention, or even a stagy bit of Gothic property. Clothing it in the poetry of words, he presents the old darkness fresh and imaginatively modern to us.

In the early short stories, especially those collected in *The October Country*, Bradbury exercises his fancy on the grotesque. He reminds us in a short prefatory comment that most of these stories were written before he was 26 and are unique to this early period of his work. Some date back to 1943. Being close to the time of Bradbury's initial introduction to and absorption in Poe's stories, these tales could well show the influence of Poe. Certainly they exhibit a sensitive use of the Gothic mode in general.

The title, *The October Country*, immediately attracts our attention. In an epigraph Bradbury describes this *country* as gloomy, more used to fogs and mists than to sunlight, more comfortable at dusk and night than at dawn and day. There one could easily suffer a day such as Poe describes in "The Fall of the House of Usher": "a dull, dark, and soundless day in the autumn of the year, when the clouds hung oppressively low in the heavens." Bradbury's October country is compartmentalized into small dark areas, the hidden places of human deprivation and depravation. His autumn people are void of hope or optimism. Occasionally one of them rouses himself for a cruel joke or last-ditch effort. But for the most part, they live static, sterile lives.

In these early stories Bradbury has heeded, intuitively or intentionally, one of Poe's often quoted lessons to those who would write prose narratives. Poe discussed the importance of unity in a review of Hawthorne's *Twice-Told Tales*, emphasizing that the short tale which dwells on terror, passion, or horror can benefit from the "certain unique or single *effect*." To avail himself of this "immense force derivable from totality," an author must choose his incidents with care.

Bradbury has added a footnote to Poe's advice, given not as a bit of literary credo but in the casual remark of one of his characters. In "The Next in Line" Marie stands looking at a pile of disjointed bones and skulls and remarks: ". . . for a thing to be horrible it has to suffer a change you can recognize." Bradbury has followed his own advice and Poe's dictum. In *The October Country* he has placed his changes against a background of familiar people, places, and activities. Many of the old Gothic conventions are present, albeit in unfamiliar guises. This perversion of accustomed twentieth-century patterns of life allow an exquisite but immense force to excite feelings of awe and dread.

Walpole's "subterraneous" regions have spawned many variations: escapeways underground, dungeons, secret vaults, catacombs with their store of ancient dead. What is more natural for a couple vacationing in Mexico than to visit one of the tourist attractions, the mummies in the local catacombs? Wired to the walls of the cavernous hall are the skeletons of those whose families could not pay the fee of a conventional burial. Joseph, a stereotypical tourist, busies himself with snapping pictures and making crude remarks about Mr. Gape and Mrs. Grimace. He even tries to buy one of the skeletons from the caretaker for a few pesos. Meanwhile, his wife Marie is responding to the human drama implicit in each "screaming" skull. When car trouble forces them to stay longer in the town, the experience works morbidly on her mind. She becomes catatonic and finally dies. Marie is a likely candidate for the "next in line." Using the familiar events of tourist travel, Bradbury has achieved low-key terror by forcing us to witness Marie's steady, seemingly inevitable disintegration into death.

Death and catacombs have become clichés in the literature of terror. Bradbury gives the cliché a fresh twist in "The Cistern," evoking a romantic melancholy instead of horror. The cistern of the title is the far-flung sewer system of a town of some 30,000 people, a town large enough to allow some of its citizens to be misplaced or go unnoticed. Because the town lies near the sea, the tides and rains flow through the system. One evening a spinster muses aloud to her sister that the cistern is actually a vast underground city. A man long dead lives there, periodically enlivened by the tides, ennobled by the waters. Anna sees him joined by a woman who has died only recently, the two forever clean and loving in their watery world. When she identifies the man as her long-lost lover, we feel a deep sadness for those whom love and gentleness have passed by. That a figure should slip out of the house later in the night and that a manhole cover should slam down seems the only melancholy solution.

Atmospheric effects, which are vital to Gothic moods, take on great importance in *The October Country*. "The Dwarf" begins on "one of those motionless hot summer nights" and ends with "large drops of hot rain" heralding a storm. "Touched with Fire" glows with heat from beginning to end: 92 degrees Fahrenheit—the temperature at which the most murders occur, the heat that sunburns, drenches with sweat, and touches off ragged tempers. The thing in "The Jar" goes with "the noiselessness of late night, and only the crickets chirping, the frogs off sobbing in the moist swamp-lands." The gathering of the weird clan in "Homecoming" occasions a host of meteorological phenomena: lightning, thunder, clammy fog, crashing rain. When Grandmama and Grandpapa arrive from the old country, they travel in a "probing, sucking tornado, funneling and nuzzling the moist night earth." Such aberrations, in the more placid weather one anticipates, adds to the mystery of the human turmoil taking place.

In "The Wind," Bradbury works atmospheric effects in an unusual way. As a central character, the wind effectively combines ancient and modern Romance. Common sense tells us that wind blows under doors, rattles windows, and slams shutters. In a high-intensity storm it can also blow down power lines and cause great property damage and human tragedy. But Brad-bury's wind is born of ancient Romance, too; it is a compendium of all the winds of the Earth, with a personality and purpose of its own.

Like Roderick Usher, "enchained by certain superstitious impressions" of his own home, in Bradbury's story Allin is enthralled by the sentience of the wind that pursues him. It laughs and whispers, then slams and crashes. It sucks and nuzzles at his house, seeking revenge on this mere mortal who dares trespass on its secret breeding and dying place in the Himalayas. Finally, it corners Allin in the house. He is isolated except for telephone contact with Herb, a rather pedestrian friend who tries to understand the situation, but cannot. When the wind turns into a feral creature with a voice compounded of the voices of the thousands killed in typhoons and hurri-canes, Herb can only listen helplessly as Allin says: "It's a killer, Herb, the biggest, damnedest prehistoric killer that ever hunted prey." A primal force, the wind sucks not only at Allin's house but at his very intellect and ego.

Not all of Bradbury's houses are places in which to hide, however. Sometimes they are fragile shells to break out of. In "Jack-in-the-Box" a young boy lives in a four-storied house effectively sealed from the world by a natural barrier (a dense grove of trees) and an artificial barrier (a mother's unnatural fear of the world). The boy exists in this four-level universe in the company of his mother and Teacher, a bespectacled, gray-gloved person dressed in a cowled robe. From Teacher he learns a story of Creation, with a dead father as God and a future role for him as son and successor. His flight to safety is through a tunnel of trees to the strange sanctuary of the world of lampposts and friendly policemen on the beat. Only when he "dies" to his old artificial world and is "reborn" in this world of the beetles that killed Father can he throw his arms aloft and be free like the jack-in-the-box.

One refreshing difference between Bradbury's use of the Gothic mode and that of many other authors is evident in his choice of characters. When one reads a considerable number of Gothic tales, the Isabellas, Adelines, and Eleanoras tend to flow together and become that abstract entity, Beauty in Distress. She remains in our minds as a white-clothed, wraith-like figure perpetually in flight, pursued by a cruel and tyrannical male. It matters little whether his name is Manfred or Montoni, Lucifer or Death. On the other hand, Bradbury's people are personalities, believable people we can care about. Not limited by sex or age, they represent Innocence in Distress, though each is unique in his innocence.

Bradbury's people do not flee, for autumn people tend to seal themselves off until a point is reached when they must act. Often their act is so aggressive and unexpected that it tinges with dismay our sympathy for their plight. We may judge their actions, but not by any conventional moral yardstick. Instead, like Poe's prisoner in "The Pit and the Pendulum," we accept them as victims of "that surprise, or entrapment into torment, [which] formed an important portion of these dungeon deaths." Like the prisoner, Bradbury's characters suffer in the dungeons of spiritual darkness where one fights against the death of spirit. The struggle may end grotesquely, even in death, though the death is often that of the tormentor rather than the tormented.

Surprise into the grotesquerie of death? What else but surprise can we feel with 11-year-old Douglas in "The Man Upstairs" when he discovers that Grandma's new boarder has a collection of triangles, chains, and pyramids instead of the standard heart, lungs, and stomach? Evidently something unhuman, more used to sleeping all day in a coffin in a dark basement, now sleeps in Grandma's upper floor. A strangeness threatens the warmth of Grandma's kitchen where she teaches the basic facts of human physiology to Douglas as she deftly stuffs a fowl for the evening meal. Bradbury inveigles us into sharing the ever-expanding curiosity of the small boy, from his initial discovery to the end. Then he jolts us into ancient Romance when we find the boarder, dechained and depyramided, neatly trussed up like a Thanksgiving turkey, stuffed with six dollars and fifty cents in silver coins.

Entrapment into torment? Take Charlie of "The Jar." Living in a shack in the Louisiana back country, Charlie has his own personal dungeon—a narrow social group where he is ridiculed and ignored. The "thing" in the jar brings him sorely needed social attention. When his wife Thedy threatens to strip it of its mystique in front of the neighbors, Charlie is trapped by a torment; he can neither face it nor flee it. Instead, he acts decisively. Later, along with his rival, Tom Carmody, a reader may shiver as he too looks at the new thing in the jar. Grotesque though it is, we grudgingly accept Thedy's end, given the menace of her vicious tongue.

Sometimes we accomplish our dungeon deaths by our own frantic efforts. What else is hypochondria but self-entrapment into torment? We flee from our dis-ease, grabbing at any proffered relief. In "Skeleton," Mr. Harris suffers acutely from aches in his bones. Gradually he becomes aware of and is then obsessed by the unwelcome skeleton that his muscles carry around day in and day out. It becomes his enemy, forcing itself out in hideous protrusions of teeth and nails. Harris's family doctor treats his problem with veiled mockery. Finally, in desperation he turns to a M. Munigant, a small dark man with glittering eyes and a sibilant voice that seems to rise in a shrill whistle. Relief at any cost, asks Mr. Harris, even that provided by M. Munigant who deftly extracts the bones from his body, leaving only a live human jellyfish.

Bradbury can turn a stock situation inside out, even invest it with a degree of humor. A standard Gothic convention is the confrontation with a supernatural force. It may be a shadowy form of a long-dead love or an ancient ancestor stepping out of his gold frame. It can appear in a mirror instead of the expected human reflection. In some tales, Satan or Death may appear in human form. With such occurrences the author is usually trying to strike a chill in the reader, as well as the character involved.

It comes as gentle relief when an author turns the tables on such apparitions. Poe did it in "Bon-Bon," when the devil rejects the soul of a gourmet-restaurateur, indicating delicately that he cannot take advantage of Bon-Bon in his drunken condition. Like Poe, Bradbury twists the classic formula. In "There Was an Old Woman" he gives us Aunt Tildy, a spry old lady with years of knitting left in her fingers. When a polite, dark young man with his four helpers carrying a long wicker basket come to her house, she becomes quite vexed with him. Losing the first part of the battle, she watches as they carry her body away to the mortuary. By dint of a will stronger than death, she forces her spirit to follow them to the mortuary where she commands it to merge with the body, to think, and then to force the body to sit up. Polite to the end, she leaves only after thanking the amazed mortician. With her homespun, no-nonsense mannerisms Aunt Tildy is a far cry from the emaciated Madeline Usher inching her way from the tomb to the room where Roderick awaits her.

While the short stories of *The October Country* amply illustrate Bradbury's ability to gothicize his plots in a unique way, the novel form clearly offers the freedom to expand and play intricate variations on the conventions. Both *Something Wicked This Way Comes* and *The Halloween Tree* demonstrate Bradbury's exercise of this freedom. Written a decade apart, they nevertheless offer certain basic similarities as a starting point for the more pertinent divergences from the Gothic mode. These basic similarities, all from Walpole's idea of modern Romance, are in the choice of characters, setting, time of year, and moral values.

As mentioned above, Bradbury replaced the customary Beauty in Distress with Innocence in Distress. In these two novels his innocents are preadolescent boys full of guileless ignorance, who count a few years as a zillion yet do not fear the march of years. They whoop, holler, and jostle for the sheer joy of moving muscles. In the next breath they may shrink, chill, and whisper at a premonition of the future. Unlike Edwin of "Jack-in-the-Box," they use the free, overhead gesture of the Jack as a natural, everyday posture.

The two novels take place at the same season of the year—Halloween. In *The Halloween Tree* it is the time for costumes and cries of "trick or treat." For Jim and Will in *Something Wicked*, it is a time of sweet anticipation, for their joint birthdays arrive with Halloween. Neither set of boys belongs to October country, that desolate, empty abode of desolate, empty people. Instead, they live in Halloween country, a land of happy illusion until some unforeseen power shakes their consciousness.

The boys do not call it Halloween country, and neither does Bradbury. Their homes are somewhere in twentieth-century Midwestern United States. In *The Halloween Tree* Bradbury plants his boys' roots firmly in a small town near a small river and small lake. No chance of a frowning Gothic edifice in a place where smallness is so decidedly emphasized. How about Green Town, Illinois, of *Something Wicked*? Green Town. The very name summons up a population of citizens proud of tree-lined streets bulwarked by lush lawns and luxuriant gardens. Could a moldering ruin find welcome in here? Probably not. In neither town is there place for the stagy, trumped-up settings of the older tales of terror and horror.

Nonetheless, mystery and wonder, awe and terror do come to both Midwestern towns. Before, during, and after the night journeys and night-marish experiences of the boys, two strong human emotions, love and loyalty, hold firm against preternatural events and portents. Embedded in the relationship of the boys and their families, as well as that of the boys and their community, these two positive energies avert tragedy and provide an unwavering reference point.

Love and loyalty stabilize the events of *Something Wicked*. The novel is fraught with polarities: dark and light, age and youth, good and evil, time and spirit, death and life. Without the fine balance of love, the poles would fly apart. Combined by loyalty, the polarities become those Blakean contraries without which "there is no progression." *Something Wicked* is also a novel of paradoxes. Why do human beings rush to grow up but fight growing old? Why do we yearn for what is not and can never be? Why does evil attract good? Even love and loyalty bring no answers; they serve only to protect each time the "cosmic fear" touches us.

William Halloway and James Nightshade epitomize both the contraries and the paradoxes. They live side by side in a quiet neighborhood of Green Town. Born only two minutes apart, separated by midnight Halloween, they share a rare kinship. They complement each other: one light, one dark; one cautious, one daring; one all impulse, the other given to thought; one untrammelled in imagination, the other touched by reason. Mutually supportive, they operate as one complex personality in two separate bodies. Both are beginning to feel those vague, then not-so-vague, yearnings toward maturity.

During the day and most of the nights these yearnings still play a minor part, second to the larger concerns of preadolescent boys. There are many streets to run down full tilt, bushes to leap, and stars to hoot at. Their homes serve them well. These are houses from which to escape down boy-known footholds. Homes in Green Town have doors that slam after boys leaving in the sunlight. Mothers smile happily in the rooms, and fathers return from work to warm their hands in front of fires.

The placid world of Green Town changes when a carnival comes to town on October 24. Its unexpected arrival, a full two months after the customary date for carnivals, affects people in different ways. Mr. Crosetti, the barber, cries a little with nostalgia at the smell of cotton candy. Miss Foley, the elderly schoolteacher, anticipates showing her nephew the sights. The boys look forward to a full engagement with all the exotic offerings of the carnival.

Despite expectations, the carnival doesn't run true to form. For one thing, it does not set up its tents in the blaze of day with a flurry of activity; it slips quietly in under cover of dark in the wee hours of morning. No brawny roustabouts tug at ropes and canvas; the personnel are limited to those normally seen only in freak sideshows. This carnival harbors a secret. During their nighttime peregrinations Will and Jim discover it, and by so doing, invite the vengeance of Mr. Dark, the proprietor. As long as they flee him together, they are safe; but he finally runs them to ground. Only love and loyalty save them—the love of a father and the loyalty of accepting one's alter ego. Others in the community lose in one way or another, for they lack these fortifying emotions.

Something Wicked This Way Comes tosses up all manner of bits and ends from the Gothic river, with its full freight of conventions, from Walpole to the present. One of the first things we notice are the supernatural elements, which Bradbury early introduces in the meeting of the boys with a salesman of lightning rods. His repetition of their names, Halloway and Nightshade, underscores their connotations. Sensing imminent storm and stress around Jim, the salesman urges a lightning rod for Jim's house. It is a rod such as never seen before in Green Town, a rod decorated with crescent and cross, scarab and "Phoenician hentracks," plus hex signs from every conceivable folk culture. As the salesman explains, a storm has no nationality. The storm he foretells turns out to be not only a meteorological phenomenon but a spiritual and psychological upheaval as well.

The episode between the salesman and the boys initiates a train of exotic and occult images, all clustered around the carnival. Its very name— Cooger & Dark's Pandemonium Shadow Show—evokes memories of Milton's Satan and the apostate angels building a rival to the City of God. The freak show advertises a Mephistopheles; a skeleton is one of the attractions. A blind Dust Witch, out of folklore fears, trails her sensitive fingertips over the roof of Jim's home as she hangs vampire-like over the basket of the moldy green balloon. The Dangling Man reminds us of the Hanged Man of the Tarot deck. The Dwarf, the Crusher, and the Lava-Drinker parody normalcy. Strapped in an electric chair and infused with electrical life is Mr. Electrico, a twentieth-century M. Valdemar sustained by galvanism rather than Poe's mesmerism.

Heading this macabre crew is Mr. Dark, that ominous "illustration-drenched, super-infested civilization of souls." Dark in appearance as well as name, he embodies all that we fear: evil, the devil, death, death-in-life. Mr. Dark is not a mocking Lucifer arriving in a "sulphurous whirlwind" as in Lewis's *The Monk*. This pock-faced man with yellow eyes quietly stalks his carnival grounds, tyrannizing his guilt-and-pain-ridden freaks. In moments of agitation or cold calculation he energizes the illustrations on his body, hypnotizing the watcher with troubled dreams. Like his entourage, Mr. Dark contributes to the brooding sense of mystery by which Bradbury progressively detaches us from everyday life.

The old Gothic backgrounds can play little part in *Something Wicked*. Where in Green Town, Illinois, are the vaults and subterraneous regions of decaying institutions to fit the Gothic demands? If we see this small town with the sensitivity of Bradbury's eyes, we can spot them. Will and Jim must hide from the fierce, penetrating eyes of the carnival people parading Main Street. Unlike Walpole's Isabella, they cannot pry up a trapdoor and run through a dark passageway to the local church. But they can pry up an iron grille covering a window well in front of the United Cigar Store. There in the cool shadows, along with discarded cigarette butts, gum wrappers, and stray pennies, they crouch in fear but, for the moment, in comparative safety.

There is no haunted, brooding house in Green Town—only the special one with the "Theater" on Hickory Street where a bedroom couple act out life with savage delight. Green Town does, however, have a quasi-Gothic pile. What else but the public library, that institution dedicated to the protection of antiquity? Here, by custom, silence reigns. Old ideas and discredited theories molder undisturbed on dusty shelves. When the library is closed, the stacks of books carry echoes as well as did Udolpho's galleries or Usher's rooms. From the shadows in the corners, Awe, Terror, and Superstition can stalk straight out of Poe into the twentieth century. This is a logical site for the illogical battle between good and evil.

Taking part in such a struggle must be a hero. A brooding bookworm Heathcliff? No. Green Town offers only the custodian, Charles Halloway, Will's father. The odds are against him, for he has only books to use against the forces of ignorance. Bradbury's modern demon of temptation, Mr. Dark, arrogantly tosses the Bible into a wastebasket and then plays with utter certainty on Charles' weakness, his awareness of the passing years. Despite the unevenness of the match, Charles makes the effort to save his innocents, like all his predecessors, the faithful deliverers of countless Gothic ladies. Like them, he loses the first tilt, but returns to win in the end.

As in Bradbury's short fiction, the atmospheric conditions in *Something Wicked* run true to Gothic form. Again, the meeting of the salesman and the boys acts as a vanguard for the impending storm; for the salesman keeps an eye out for the savage disturbance coming on his very heels. The wind blows warm, then cold, carrying on it the comforting smell of cotton candy, as well as the high eerie tones of the carousel. Strangely enough, the music plays backward, and the aroma exists only in old, nostalgic memory. When the storm finally breaks, it does so in dreadful sublimity, with loud thunder and hard rain that rouses the carousel to "malodorous streams of music." Frightening events occur in the darkness. The carnival slips in at three in the morning. Miss Foley disintegrates in the depths of her shadowy house and later, under the rainy shadows of an oak tree, sobs for her lost self. Mr. Dark and Charles Halloway have their calamitous meeting beneath a single light bulb in an otherwise unlit library.

Along with the Gothic conventions of place and atmospherics, Bradbury has used effects that Poe might have called *arabesque*. These are designed to detach still further the characters and readers from those familiar reference points of time, space and ego. Like a great wheel of fortune, the carousel can throw a rider off in a different state of being, older or younger. As it splinters light into myriad artificial gleams, the mirror maze throws back cold reflections to warm bodies. In the freak tent Mr. Dark throws the switch, and Mr. Cooger metamorphoses into a blue, then green, sizzling, flickering electrical display. When he is agitated, Mr. Dark's illustrated body swarms with kaleidoscopic variety. In every distortion of the normal a terrible beauty is born, exciting and attracting, yet offering nothing for something.

With its surrealistic impact, the arabesque technique fosters mystery and wonder. It also affords the author the opportunity to insinuate moral and psychological questions. Usually one enters a mirror maze to enjoy the distortions of the normal, everyday image; but the maze can destroy a fragile ego when it reflects "a multifold series of empty vanities." What responsibility do we have for the Miss Foleys of the world who see in the mirror maze only multiple images of a faded self, an aging replica of one's self-image? While intuitively avoiding the maze after one encounter, Jim and Will try to save the weaker Miss Foley by discouraging her visit there; but she goes and is destroyed. Charles Halloway, in contrast, shrinks from entering the maze, knowing what he must face. Unlike Miss Foley, he knows himself and has accepted his aging body and spirit. By so doing, he can run the gamut of the mirror to save the boys.

A novel in the Gothic style can be tested by the fine balance which the author has maintained between the ancient and modern Romance (to recall Walpole's terms). Has he blended imagination and improbability with adherence to the common life? A very real trap lies in the subtle fascination of the ancient Romance. How easily the author can be lured to blot out the real with the surreal, or bury the characters under a mountain of grotesque events. At some point the sensitive writer must relieve both characters and readers from fear and terror while retaining a sense of the wonderful.

Ray Bradbury recognizes the need for this return to the light of day. In *Something Wicked* Charles Halloway is Bradbury's vehicle for this return. Bereft of the expected strength of ancient wisdom in books, Charles falls back on himself. Physically, he cannot match the attraction of evil, especially the attraction it has for Jim Nightshade. Psychologically, Charles is enervated by having to face the fact of his own mortality; with the recognition, however, comes acceptance. Giving up in defeat won't do. But standing firm and celebrating life, even with its fears and weaknesses, will. Charles Halloway laughs, and by doing so, forces the boys to laugh. Laughter heals wounds and restores equilibrium. What does it matter that the laughter is bittersweet with the knowledge that victory is temporary? The "autumn people" will return; temptation will always be active in one guise or another. On the other side of the ledger, growth brings strength. With each new year, Will and Jim will grow stronger until they can cope with the "autumn people" on their own. By showing them the foolishness of attaching too much or too little importance to the dark side of man's nature, Charles

Halloway has bequeathed them a healing gift. At the same time Bradbury has discharged the Gothic convention of restoring moral and social order.

The Halloween Tree offers us quite different fare. At first glance it appears to be fantasy devoid of Gothic overtones. Take the delightful customs of an American Halloween. All children enjoy them, and most adults rediscover the joy each time there is a knock at the door on the night of October 31. The cry of "trick or treat" and the masking of ordinary faces behind boldly colored paper ones have become beloved clichés. Few of us question the origin of these yearly rites, and even fewer would take seriously any intimation of superstition at work here.

The Halloween Tree presents the thesis that behind the gay voices and weird costumes, a very real fear is at work. It is the fear of loss of light which translates ultimately into death. *The Halloween Tree* confronts us with the fear as Bradbury surprises us with a surface-light but soul-deep history of the origin and growth of Halloween superstitions. The lesson is not difficult to take, for it assumes the guise of an airy fantasy, deceptively taught to eight 12-year-old pals who congregate on the holiday to do the usual things. When they stop to collect Pipkin, a special person to all of them, he appears ill but promises to meet them at "the House." Reassured, they head for the appointed place. Down a dark ravine, full of night rustlings and pungent odors of long-decayed life, they plunge, finally pulling up short before the place of the Haunts.

Many small Midwestern towns can boast of at least one haunted house, probably built around the turn of the century, possibly by the first affluent member of the original family in the area. If not, there is certainly the home of an elderly eccentric, a house to which small boys are never admitted but whose blank windows, high eaves, and weathered siding draw them like a magnet. Such a house is the Haunts. It promised welcome chills with its "gummed-shut doors." Myriad chimneys rose like cemetery markers from the peaked roof-top. When stepped on, the planks of the front porch screeched with ghostly music. Most pleasurably fearful of all, the front door had a Marley knocker to summon up all the Christmas ghosts of Dickens two full months ahead of time.

As Tom Skelton, he behind the skeleton mask, cracked the knocker, his friends, safe behind masks of mummy, witch, beggar, and all, crouched behind him. The front door flew open in true Gothic style, untouched by human hands. "Darkness moved within darkness," and then a voice from a tall, shadowy figure rejected their "treat" and demanded a "trick." After abjuring the customary ritual of Halloween, Carapace Clavicle Mound-shroud proceeds to whirl the eight boys back to the Past, the Undiscovered Country, and uncover the darkness and nightmare that lies there.

In the few hours before midnight releases them into All Saints' Day, the boys travel back in time and around in space. They experience ten thousand years of the growth of superstition, beginning with Neolithic man crowding his fire and fearing the death of the sun. They climb the pyramids in ancient Egypt at the time when the Osiris legend personified the same fear. They share in a Greek Feast of the Pots, a festival of the dead which prefigures Mexico's *El Día de los Muertos.* On both occasions the living seek to propitiate shades of the departed with food and attention. As druidic priests try their form of propitiation, the eight boys watch Samhain out of the mists of Celtic myth scythe down human souls. They hover over secret bonfires, watching the rise of witchcraft flourishing even as Christianity conquers the old pagan religions. Comes the time when Notre Dame is to be built to the glory of God. They aid in the building of the cathedral, whose every pinnacle is encrusted with monstrous forms and gargoyles to testify to the church's recognition of the vices, sins, and illusions that torment humankind.

In all this childlike fantasy and adventure, the Gothic machinery is efficiently at work. The subterraneous passage appears as the long tunnel into the center of a pyramid where the small Egyptian Pipkin is laid with toys, food, and possessions. It reappears centuries later with the opening of the trapdoor to the Mexican catacombs, complete with its 104 mummies, waiting for the Mexican Pipkin to join them. Out of the witch cults branch those many secret societies of the later German horror romances. In the transformation of sins and outmoded gods into stone gargoyles, Bradbury has added to the stable of spectral manifestations from which Gothic writers draw. As Moundshroud explains, "All the old gods, all the old dreams, all the old nightmares, all the old ideas with nothing to do, out of work, we *gave* them work."

Even Death materializes. Bradbury's Carapace Clavicle Moundshroud differs significantly from the many dark-cowled figures or shadowy threats in the long stretches of Gothic hallways. His Death is a genial schoolmaster, teaching patiently but thoroughly. Early in their association, Moundshroud questions the boys about their masks and costumes. Why was this one wearing a skull, that one dressed like a gargoyle? Why had the one over there swathed himself in surgical gauze like a mummy? In their amazed silence he answers his own question with "you don't *really* know!" In teaching them to know, to really know, he reverses the roles by "tricking" them into giving up one year of each of their lives that their friend Pipkin may have the "treat" of life now.

The educational travels to which Moundshroud treats the boys are pure arabesque in design. They swirl in time and space, clinging to a pterodactyl-like kite which is made of a collage of fierce animal eyes. Linked together, the eight of them form the tail of the kite whipping through the eons. At the end of the lesson they return to the present in the vortex of a cyclonic wind. There are other images of fusion and separation. Before their eyes, Mr. Moundshroud explodes into a swarm of leaves, only to gather himself again in a voice centuries and miles away. Their friend Pipkin sustains a continual process of metempsychosis as centuries and places shift. Beside the House, the Halloween Tree stands festooned with pumpkin smiles which resolve into a sea of human faces and then, as lights go out one by one, the very winds speak with human voices.

The universe of *The Halloween Tree* is protean. Each change stimulates a renascence of wonder as familiar forms acquire new identities without losing their fundamental meanings. Amid these ever-shifting realities only the eight boys, united by love and loyalty for Pipkin, provide a steady reference point.

When John Ruskin formulated his six "moral elements" of Gothic architecture in 1854, he insisted on examining internal elements contributed by the builders. He identified these as "certain mental tendencies of the builders, legibly expressed in it [Gothic architecture]: as fancifulness, love of variety, love of richness and others." For Ruskin these mental powers were equal in importance to the external form. He emphasized this duality:

> It is not enough that it has the Form, if it have not also the power and life. It is not enough that it has the Power, if it have not the Form.

This dictum also can apply to the art of building fiction in the Gothic mode. It is not enough that the author of fiction be master of the Gothic themes and conventions, if he has not the creative imagination to invest them with power and life.

Bradbury has demonstrated his power to discipline and give new life to selected forms in the Gothic tradition. In some stories of *The October Country* he savages the complacency with which we accept social veneer as reality by forcing us to accept the grotesquerie of those lives whose veneer has worn thin. In *Something Wicked This Way Comes* he invests the forms with a power that causes us to mistrust the even tenor of our individual and communal existence. Even as we are disturbed, we accept the naturalness of the situation.

Ruskin's love of change operates to the same ends as Poe's arabesque—that perception of the "half-closed eye" which blurs hard outlines into multiple realities. Both *Something Wicked* and *Halloween* are evidence of

Bradbury's power to infuse illusions and delusions with life. Paradoxically, unity exists in multiplicity even as sensuous experiences elude the harness of reason. Over it all, Bradbury throws the power of poetry, giving his ideas and images a rich verbal treatment to which we might assign Ruskin's word, *Generosity*. With his "fancifulness, love of variety, love of richness and others," Bradbury has successfully blended the ancient and modern Romance.

LAHNA DISKIN

Bradbury on Children

"*The reason why grownups and kids fight is because they belong to separate races. Look at them, different from us. Look at us, different from them.*" So writes twelve-year-old Douglas Spaulding in his first journal. It is a truth central not only to the summer of 1928 in *Dandelion Wine* but to Ray Bradbury's general view of children. To trace the unfolding of this truth in his fiction, I will focus on two novels, *Dandelion Wine* and *Something Wicked This Way Comes,* as well as several short stories.

Early in *Dandelion Wine* Tom Spaulding wonders why his older brother wants to record "new crazy stuff" in a "yellow nickel tablet." Succinctly, Douglas explains his reason for preserving his special observations:

> "I'm alive."
> "Heck, that's old!"
> "*Thinking* about it, *noticing* it, is new. You do things and don't watch. Then all of a sudden you look and see what you're doing and it's the first time, really. . . ."

He goes on to say that his record is in two parts. The first is called "RITES AND CEREMONIES" and the second "DISCOVERIES AND REVELATIONS or maybe ILLUMINATIONS, that's a swell word, or INTUITIONS, okay?" These

From *Ray Bradbury*. © 1980 by Martin Harry Greenberg and Joseph D. Olander.

headings are more than felicitous keynotes for what will happen to and around the boys during the summer; they suggest conditions of existence and signify operations in the ethos of children—children as a different species. For example, the boys in Bradbury's two novels consecrate their friendship with diversions, often secret, which grow into private systems of symbols. Often in the form of ceremonies, these systems insulate them from the restrictions and machinations of adults. The rituals and discoveries, together with the revelations and illuminations, enable Bradbury's children to cross boundaries that separate reality and fantasy. They come and go from one domain to the other, and often unite the two. If we grant that reality and fantasy are cultures, then children have the idiopathic ability to cross cultures. While this kind of traffic may be second nature to some adults, it is first nature to children. In their passage between dimensions, the children in Bradbury's fiction, not always benignly and often intentionally, overstep society's norms. They sanction certain actions and behavior which they know to be outlawed by society. Sometimes murder is the kind of freedom practiced by members of Bradbury's separate race.

With libidinous joy, Bradbury's boys share the events of human life with the adults in their families and communities. But their sharing differs in quality from that of their parents and townspeople. Their fix on the phenomena comprising day-to-day existence is charged with meanings which they construe from lore and legend, from myth and imagination. Re-creation, in its most inventive sense, is their daily enterprise. At times, the very air they breathe is compounded of wonder and magic, a potent elixir that transforms even the seasons of the year—summer in the case of *Dandelion Wine* and autumn in *Something Wicked This Way Comes*. For them, being alive means perceiving phenomena with an openness and acceptance by which natural processes are transmuted and turn miraculous or portentous. They rambunctiously perpetuate the freedom of childhood. Even when they behave maliciously, they are obeying their own credo, their own laws, which decree that they resist the inexorable transformation they will undergo when they migrate to adulthood. Their most outrageous actions are instinctive ploys against the inevitable doomsday of exile from childhood. Thus, in both books, the boys live at the quick of life, marauding each moment. They are afire with ecstatic temporality, resplendent immediacy.

Douglas and Tom Spaulding—along with their friends, John Huff and Charlie Woodman, in *Dandelion Wine*—live in a different zone, or season, of boyhood from that inhabited by James Nightshade and William Halloway in *Something Wicked This Way Comes*. Nevertheless, they share their origins as members of a separate race. In the truest sense of their attributes, they are creatures of a world, a secondary state, both within and beyond the planet they cohabit with their parents and other grownups. The significance of being *within* and *beyond* is that they are attuned to the higher and lower ranges of the phenomena of nature and the mysteries of the supernatural. The innocence of Bradbury's children is also part of their secondary state, for it is an estate of sanctuary and sometimes unholy sanctity. To be innocent in the context of Bradbury's fiction is to be uninhibited in imaginative daring, regardless of the consequences. When they participate in the activities of home and town, his young characters abide within a wholesome worldliness. When they venture outside those circles, they cross over into a beyond that is often sinister, a forbidding but still enticing supra-worldliness. As commuters between the two dimensions, they try to relate the different conditions of life in each, "make sense of the interchange." In *Dandelion Wine* their coordinate worlds are symbolized by the town and the ravine, each struggling at some "indefinable place" to "possess a certain avenue, a dell, a glen, a tree, a bush."

Invariably, Bradbury's boys are full of urgent emotions and are generally conscience-free. They are alternately generous and greedy, benevolent and cruel. Withal, they represent integrated, untrammeled, unpremeditated self-expression. They excel at magnifying people, places and events. Their mental extravagance can be viewed as their peculiar racial talent for enhancement.

Bradbury's principle of enhancement makes his boys kin to the spirit that pervades much of e. e. cummings' poetry. Indeed, there is an affinity between the poet's view of life and his license with language and syntax, and Bradbury's children and their license with time. In affirming that he is alive and often alone, cummings manipulates temporal relationships and diminishes fixity in form. Similarly, Bradbury's boys are devout libertarians, because their "spirit's ignorance"—hence innocence—eclipses "every wisdom knowledge fears to dare." They dare whatever must be ventured to play out their fantasies. Never halfhearted, they are creatures "whose vision can create the whole," who are "free into the beauty of the truth." Significantly, the truths they sometimes find have beauty which only they can behold. As members of a separate race, they are "citizens of ecstasies more steep than climb can time with all his years." The idea in this line of poetry applies to Bradbury's concept of children, while cummings' technique applies to their way of stalling time. The inversion of subject and verb, with *can* intervening, is an arrangement suggesting almost incessant movement or activity accompanied by equilibrium. In exchanging places, *climb* and *time* exchange functions to suggest restless equation. There is a sense of alternation and reciprocity in the tempo of a romp, to forestall the irreversible course of linear time. Like cummings' citizen, Bradbury's boys buck the tyranny of the clock. They turn with the sun and moon, plundering the days of summer in *Dandelion Wine* and the nights of autumn in *Something Wicked This Way Comes*. Too busy to capitulate, the boys in both books chase life and death and celebrate the mystique of both. For all the children in Bradbury's fiction, "everything happens that can't be done." True to cummings' sense of life, the ears of their ears awake, the eyes of their eyes are opened. They are continually poised to find "treasures of reeking innocence" and move among "such mysteries as men do not conceive."

In *Dandelion Wine* Douglas and Tom Spaulding celebrate the arrival of summer with certain simple family ceremonies. On his first excursion of the season with Tom and his father for fox grapes and wild strawberries, Douglas is seized by an overwhelming and inexplicable force: "the terrible prowler, the magnificent runner, the leaper, the shaker of souls. . . ." His startled awareness is an epiphany, a connection, a communication with the natural world. Through every inch and fiber of his body, he knows that he is a creature of Earth, a vibrant strand in what Shelley saw as the great "web of being."

Still reminiscent of Shelley, this time his skylark, Douglas is like an "unbodied joy whose race has just begun." The experience is tumultuous, dizzying, and it cannot be shared with his father. Douglas has what Shelley described in his essay, "On Life," as a "distinct and intense apprehension" of the natural world in relation to himself. He feels (to pursue Shelley's theory) as though his nature "were dissolved into the surrounding universe or as if the surrounding universe were absorbed into his being." Suddenly he is privy to a spirit world in which his embodied but seemingly personified emotions are manifested psychologically. The scene suggests the way in which the boy's emotions and the processes of nature become symbolic entities unto themselves, spirits and demi-spirits. Douglas's great burst of psychic energy has the power to become an almost visible presence projecting itself into the outside world. This dramatic presence is both noumenal and extra-noumenal, in that Douglas both conceives of and perceives the phenomena that possess him. The connection between the boy and animate nature gives him the sense of potent and splendid interrelatedness, as well as autonomy. Finding his identity in the woodland sense world, he extols his self-affirmation with utter abandon. In the passage on pages 9–10 of *Dandelion Wine*, Bradbury evokes the notion of Douglas's emotional and spiritual immersion in a green molecular music within the multitudes of sunlit leaves and blades of grass. The almost audible and felt hum of slow sap inside everything that grows pulses invisibly and harmonizes with Douglas's lyric blood. As he counts "the twin hearts beating in each ear, the third heart beating in his throat, the two hearts throbbing his wrists, the real heart pounding in his chest," his internal manifesto catches the mystic integration between himself and planet Earth. It is the private rhapsody of his soul's sacrament in nature with its power to intensify or raise his consciousness of life. The importance of Douglas's summer baptism is that, for Bradbury, it is an experience reserved for children. All of Bradbury's boy characters have the potential for the ordeal and the initiation because, as a race, children live in a state of readiness for the verities and illuminations of their manifest sensations.

The parents in Bradbury's stories are another breed. As such, they have lost the capacity to attend to and follow their sensations. Habit and workday concerns have dulled them to the imaginative dimensions they once frequented as children. The impedimenta of adulthood change one's outlook and impair his capacity to apprehend the world openly with keen, clear senses. Age can clog or even close the channels between man and nature. Bradbury hints that Mr. Spaulding was once like his son. In *Something Wicked This Way Comes*, Mr. Halloway is a somewhat forlorn character, gently envious of his son's singular endowments as a member of a race he can only dimly, if at all, remember as his own.

In Bradbury's canon, children are, by contrast, agents who can transfigure and sometimes metamorphose persons, things, and events. They are, in other words, apostles of enhancement. In *Dandelion Wine*, dandelions, snowflakes, shoes, and rugs are some of the elements they use. For the Spaulding boys, gathering the dandelions for wine is no ordinary chore. The essence of summer is the dandelion wine, crocked and bottled and sequestered in "cellar gloom." It is a precious potion that perpetuates the season long after it would have otherwise passed into oblivion. As summertime reincarnated and resurrected, it is a sovereign remedy for winter miseries. The boys believe that it is as life-giving as the season from which it comes. They plunge into the sea of dandelions, awash in the golden splendor. To Douglas's mind, all the ingredients of the brew are consecrated, even rain-barrel water, like "faintly blue silk" that "softened the lips and throat and heart."

Tom shares his brother's capacity for enhancement. In the midst of Douglas's contact with "the Thing," and in contrast to his secret silent communion, Tom proclaims his own right to glory for having preserved a February snowflake in a matchbox: "I'm the only guy in all Illinois who's got a snowflake in summer. . . . Precious as diamonds, by gosh." Tom's broadcast is like a badge of honor in full view. Douglas fears that Tom's excitement will scare off the Thing. Then he realizes that the presence was not only unafraid of Tom but that "Tom drew it with his breath . . . was part of it!"

The notion of enhancement also applies to Douglas's determination to have new sneakers. Bradbury's boys are adventure-bound in feet bared to summer's textures and tempos or shod in "Cream-Sponge Para Litefoot Shoes." Douglas knows that for the exploits of Summer 1928, last year's lifeless, threadbare sneakers will never do. After all, a knight is not a knight without his jambeaus and sollerets, just as the boys of summer in Green Town, Illinois, are not ready for "June and the earth full of raw power and everything everywhere in motion" without new sneakers. Douglas believes that the Para Litefoot brand can be an antigravity device for jumping over fences, sidewalks, dogs—even rivers, trees, and houses. "The magic was always in the new pair of shoes," ready to transform him into antelope or gazelle.

Rug-cleaning is an annual family event which undergoes enhancement. It sounds like an authentic ritual complete with coven, when Bradbury says: "These great wire wands were handed around so they stood, Douglas, Tom, Grandma, Great-grandma, and Mother poised like a collection of witches and familiars over the dusty patterns of old Armenia." Amid the "intricate scrolls and loops, the flowers, the mysterious figures, the shuttling patterns," Tom sees not only a parade of fifteen years of family life but pictures of the future as well. All he needs to do, especially at night under the lamplight, is adjust his eyes and peer around at the warp and woof and even the underskin.

The encounters of several children, including Tom and old lonely Helen Bentley, are the best evidence in *Dandelion Wine* of the time gulf between two different races, children and adults. Mrs. Bentley is dislocated in time; thus she is a displaced person. Isolated by choice in her widowhood, she has never accepted the fact that time is irredeemable. Instead she is caught in the backwater of carefree, loving years as a child, a young woman, and a wife. Consigning life to yesterday, she has sacrificed both the present and the future, which have little substance or reality for her. Little Jane and Alice, Tom Spaulding's playmates, find her ensconced, even engulfed, among the mementos of a lifetime. Denying that she was ever their age, they accuse her of stealing the treasures she shows them. The comb she wore when she was nine, the ring she wore when she was eight, her picture at seven—all are discredited and then confiscated by the heartless children. When she is frustrated in her attempts to authenticate a past which means everything to her, she accepts a bittersweet truth "Oh, God, children are children, old women are old women, and nothing in between. They can't imagine a change they can't see." She summons her husband's spirit to save her from despair. Consoled, she realizes that he would have agreed with the girls: "Those children are right. . . . They stole nothing from you, my dear. Those things don't belong to you *here*, you *now*. They belonged to her, that other you, so long ago." Long years after her husband's wisdom and death, she discovers that time is a trickster. It gulls the young with delusions of permanence. To the children who frolic about her and taunt her, change is a hoax; they will not allow it to intrude on their eternal Now. The people who inhabit their present are immanent. Understanding the children's fix on time, Helen Bentley acquiesces by disposing of her pictures, affidavits, and trinkets—the superfluity of a lifetime. Thereby, the erstwhile sentimentalist divests herself of the stultifying past. She resigns herself to the present and submits to the unrelenting ridicule of the intransigent children. With no trace of moral solicitude, they persist. In the closing dialogue of the chapter, Bradbury shows Jane and Alice as adamant persecutors:

> "How old are you, Mrs. Bentley?"
> "Seventy-two."
> "How old were you fifty years ago?"
> "Seventy-two."
> "You weren't ever young, were you, and never wore ribbons or dresses like these?"
> "No."
> "Have you got a first name?"
> "My name is Mrs. Bentley."
> "And you always lived in this one house?"
> "Always."
> "And never were pretty?"
> "Never."
> "Never in a million trillion years?"
> . . . .
> "Never," said Mrs. Bentley, "in a million trillion years."

Equally unenlightened, Douglas and Tom conclude that "old people never *were* children!" Saddened by their unreasonable doubt, they decide that "there's nothing we can do to help them."

In the case of Helen Bentley, the children are skeptics of anything that contradicts the reality of their immediate perceptions. No matter what she claims and has to back up her claims, they discount it as belying appearances. In the case of Colonel Freeleigh, however, they are willing to suspend disbelief. A relic like Helen Bentley, he is sick and dying. But it isn't his declining health that accounts for the difference in the way Douglas and his friends respond to him. They compromise or extend their credulity for him because they associate him with far-off places and high adventure. Naive and eager for vicarious exploits, the boys enter Colonel Freeleigh's house and his presence to sit at his feet and hear him recount the bizarre events of his life. His vivid extrapolations from American history beguile them as he holds his small audience captive with stagey accounts of oriental magic, Pawnee Bill and the bison, and the Civil War. Capricious and egocentric, the boys dismiss Helen Bentley as a fraud while at the same time mythologizing Colonel Freeleigh. In fact, he becomes their human time machine. Douglas even decides that their discovery, the "Colonel Freeleigh Express," belongs in his journal. His entry shows an inconsistency and an ingenuous lack of logic which typify his "race":

> ". . . 'Maybe old people were never children, like we claim with Mrs. Bentley but big or little some of them were standing around at Appomattox the summer of 1865.' They got Indian vision and can sight back further than you and me will ever sight ahead."

Jane and Alice reject the chance to travel back into Helen Bentley's romantic past, but Douglas and his friends become regular time travelers with Colonel Freeleigh. Bradbury may be suggesting that the girls are too young for the vicarious excursions in which the boys indulge. Three or four years in age may explain Douglas's capacity to appreciate the colonel. Still, he underestimates Helen Bentley as yet another vehicle for adventure. The girls and boys alike exhibit a form of casual opportunism inherent in members of their race.

Some of Bradbury's boys possess exemplary talents. Generally, these are a variety of strenuous physical arts performed outdoors. The children he depicts are in their glory when, unconfined, they challenge any terrain with their arms and legs and voices. Joe Pipkin in *The Halloween Tree* is the newest model of his separate race. One of nine boys in the story, he is impresario of the band's escapades. Fleet, irrepressible, and altogether earthspun, he is a joyous "assemblage of speeds, smells, textures; a cross section of all the boys who ever ran, fell, got up, and ran again." He becomes the symbolic and elusive victim in a series of travels in time and space when his friends seek the origins of All Saints' Day. In the literal story line, Joe is hospitalized with acute appendicitis; but on the figurative level, he is surrealistically embroiled in the rituals which his friends witness under the auspices of the magical Mr. Moundshroud. Although Joe is always precariously reincarnated in different countries across different ages, he is a free spirit who, though melodramatically endangered, is ultimately invincible. Bradbury makes him central to the story through recurring appearances by means of supernatural projection. The description of Joe is pertinent, since Pipkin typifies Bradbury's exceptional boys, whose prowess and gallantry distinguish them among their peers:

> Joe Pipkin was the greatest boy who ever lived. The grandest boy who ever fell out of a tree and laughed at the joke. The finest

boy who ever raced around the track, winning, and then, seeing his friends a mile back somewhere, stumbled and fell, waited for them to catch up, and joined breast to breast, breaking the winner's tape. The jolliest boy who ever hunted out the haunted houses in town, which are hard to find, and came back to report on them and take all the kids to ramble through the basements and scramble up the ivy outside-bricks and shout down the chimneys and make water off the roofs, hooting and chimpanzee-dancing and ape-bellowing. The day Joe Pipkin was born all the Orange Crush and Nehi soda bottles in the world fizzed over; and joyful bees swarmed countrysides to sting maiden ladies. On his birthdays, the lake pulled out from the shore in midsummer and ran back with a tidal wave of boys, a big leap of bodies and a downcrash of laughs.

What is interesting here is how Bradbury interlaces his account of Joe's classic boyhood skills and charms with fanciful parallels. His method of idealizing Joe is consistent with the way the characters themselves romanticize their lives.

Joe Pipkin's prototype is John Huff in *Dandelion Wine*. Like his later counterpart, John excels at a variety of things. To his friend, Douglas Spaulding, he is a prince graced with goodness and generosity. At the beginning of the chapter in which Douglas learns that John will move away, Bradbury catalogs John's versatility—the arts and accomplishments that the other boys his age admire and envy. He makes it clear that boys like Huff and Pipkin are true worthies, deserving of awe and emulation. They are blithe spirits who rejoice in their openheartedness, vitality, and youth. Their overt alliance with others of their race and nature is their *joie de vivre*. Generically elite by virtue of their boyhood, they defy temporal and terrestrial realities in their play. They sport on the threshold where fabulous fictions burst into psychic wonderworks. John Huff and his kind romp in the very hub of time, spending their energy without reservation. The following passage is like a paean in which Bradbury exalts John as champion stock and makes him legendary:

He could pathfind more trails than any Choctaw or Cherokee since time began, could leap from the sky like a chimpanzee from a vine, could live underwater two minutes and slide fifty yards downstream from where you last saw him. The baseballs you pitched him he hit in the apple trees, knocking down harvests. He could jump six-foot orchard walls, swing up branches faster and come down, fat with peaches, quicker than anyone else in the gang. He ran laughing. He sat easy. He was not a bully. He was kind. His hair was dark and curly and his teeth were white as cream. He remembered the words to all the cowboy songs and would teach you if you asked. He knew the names of all the wild flowers and when the moon would rise and set and when the tides came in and out. He was, in fact, the only god living in the whole of Green Town, Illinois, during the twentieth century that Douglas Spaulding knew of.

John's imminent departure makes him notice things he missed during all the years he lived in Green Town. For instance, the first time he really pays attention to the stained-glass window in the Terle house he is frightened. The thought of all the other things he may have missed makes him panicky and sad, afraid he will forget everything he ever knew in his hometown after he has left. The point of noticing reiterates the attitude of awareness that serves as the keynote of the novel when Douglas begins his notebook. Thus Douglas learns the color of John's eyes on the brink of separation.

There is precious little time left for the two friends to share. Believing he can outwit time, Douglas wants to defer the inevitable farewells. He persuades himself that the best way to stop time is to stand still, for time, he knows instinctively, moves in and with him. He and John can stay together if they will only linger, stop moving, stretch the minutes in shared silence. Run and romp, and time is squandered; tarry, and the clock can be controlled. Later, when Douglas and his friends play statues, John is immobilized for a few minutes and becomes the object of Douglas's close scrutiny. Bradbury turns his last long look into another hymn of praise. Not even the rules of the game can stop the course of time, though. When the sound of John's running mingles with the sound of Douglas's pounding heart, they are lost to each other. Feeling abandoned and betrayed, Douglas, "cold stone and very heavy," knows only anger and hurt. Because he cannot accept the loss, he repudiates John for his desertion. By having Douglas disown John for his involuntary departure, Bradbury shows again how immanence prevails for members of his separate race.

A few, singular townspeople—such as Clara Goodwater who uses spells, wax dolls, a elixirs, and dreamer Leo Auffmann who wants to invent a "Happiness Machine"—mixed liberally with the imaginations of Douglas and Tom Spaulding, equals the elements of bizarre and memorable events. If the events are ongoing and inexplicable, the boys are all the more delighted. The evil Lonely One is their favorite until, to their dismay, Lavinia Nebbs dispels the mystery. On the same night that yet another woman becomes the victim of someone the townspeople have named the Lonely One, Lavinia stabs an intruder in her home. Everyone except the boys believe he is the killer. When the police pronounce the case closed, the delicious terror of a murderer at large ends for the boys. At first they feel bereft of their villain. The thrill of the spooky, unseen stalker has been destroyed. As long as he was alive and lurking about town in the deep of night, danger and doom in the wake of his appearance were their perverse delight. He gave them something scary to talk about. With fear and sudden death in their midst, Green Town had an element of excitement. Since Lavinia's desperate act of self-preservation, however, the town has turned dreary, like "vanilla junket," according to Charlie Woodman. This unwelcome change evokes the boys' special powers of enhancement. It is Tom Spaulding who retaliates and persuades the other boys that the intruder was a case of mistaken identity. Reality merges with illusion, fact with fancy, when he refuses to believe that the nondescript man dead in Lavinia's house is the dreaded Lonely One. After all, the stranger waiting for Lavinia "looked like a *man*"—to be exact, "like the candy butcher down front the Elite Theater nights." As Tom conjures up the scoundrel he chooses to perpetuate as Lonely One, we find the influence of the classic horror story. In conversation with his brother and Charlie Woodman, he insists that the real Lonely One is tall, gaunt, and pale with "big eyes bulging out, green eyes, like a cat." Anyone "little and red-faced and kind of fat" with sparse sandy hair, like the intruder, will never do. Thus when the glamour of the Lonely One is threatened, the boys are reduced, though only temporarily, to the commonplace. Natural sensationalists, they must spice the otherwise bland social scene. Morality, then, isn't an issue. Justice and personal safety are inconsequential when they find their fantasy lives in jeopardy.

Douglas and his friends are inhabitants of two separate milieus, each with distinct geographic features, each the stage for different pursuits. One is the community of Green Town with its homes, stores, churches, and schools, a safe and conventional domain of people engaged in predictable public and private lives. The other is the sequestered ravine abounding in secret possibilities for adventures, for rites and ceremonies observed only by children. Each area, a discrete and organic network of life, is the adversary of the other; each is jealous of its territory and dominion. For Douglas, each domain represents a different set of values, each with a powerful sanction allying him to its laws and conditions of existence. In town he participates in rites and ceremonies of the kind already discussed but which are ordained by adults. There he is a subject bound by the restraints of civilization, by an order he had nothing to do with creating. Bradbury makes us privy to his activities in the fellowship of parents and townspeople. We watch him gather fruits and dandelions, help Grandpa hang the porch swing, and help the women clean the rugs. But when he disappears into the ravine, we do not follow. Neither Bradbury nor we as readers penetrate the sanctity of the ravine where Douglas and the other boys go in defiance of parental authority and general community taboos.

We can only guess at the games and escapades played out in the seclusion of the ravine. There the boys abandon themselves to the Marvellian ideal of green thoughts in a green shade—then greenness of invention and the greenness of nature untouched by humanity. The ravine is the uncontaminated wilderness unchanged by people with their penchant for taming, landscaping, and redesigning nature. Unassailable, it is no-man's-land to the people of Green Town. They have persuaded themselves that it is a dimension within their midst, as untampered with as it is undocile, that should remain untrespassed by anything not native to it.

It may well be that Douglas and the other children are native to the ravine. They enter devil-may-care to pursue their devilment. Within its range, adults have been murdered. The children, nonetheless, come and go in charmed safety. We are left outside where, on the borders of its heavy presence, we can sense its plants and animals. Bradbury denies us the exact details of shapes and shades and deals instead in densities. Obscurity is his dramatic mode for enhancing a dimension reserved for his race of children. The ravine has outlived its colors, colors which Bradbury does not name or show as such, instead enveloping them with invisibility and anonymity. The vegetation, animals, and insects are beyond us, too recessed to see. We are confronted with an intense statis—a vast, deep, above all impenetrable, aliveness that is both alluring and forbidding. This receding intensity and mystery bestow on Bradbury's ravine an aura of agelessness and venerability. Embedded within its depths are secret processes and life forces with the gargantuan capacity for renascence.

One evening Douglas is in the ravine later than usual. Besieged by fear, his mother takes Tom to hunt for him. For the first time in his life Tom experiences the helplessness and isolation, the utter terror, at the prospect of death encroaching on their lives. He is riddled with all the fears his fertile imagination can produce. Still, they head for the ravine:

> He could smell it. It had a dark-sewer, rotten-foliage, thick-green odor. It was a wide ravine that cut and twisted across town—a jungle by day, a place to let alone at night, Mother often declared.

The awesome nighttime power of the ravine coalesces into an almost animate thing, an entity that concentrates its jungle spirit toward a climax, "tensing, bunching together its black fibers, drawing in power from sleeping countrysides all about, for miles and miles." Tom knows that in the menacing darkness and thick silence they are poised on the brink of either Douglas's annihilation or his salvation. Suddenly, as in defiance of what seem to Tom to be demonic elements of possession, a trinity of laughing innocents appears. Douglas, John Huff, and Charlie Woodman emerge as scapegraces, for clinging to their bodies and clothes are the nameless rank odors as well as magic aromas of the ravine. Many days and nights will pass before soap, water, and other civilized hygienic measures wash away and annul the interlude in the ravine where the boys were creatures of the wild.

Besides the ravine, Summer's Ice House and the arcade are favorites of the boys. The arcade in particular can ward off Douglas's unusual morbid thoughts of his own mortality. It is a fantasy world "completely set in place, predictable, certain, sure." Best of all, its various attractions—the robot, the gorilla, the Keystone Kops, the Wright brothers, Teddy Roosevelt, Madame Tarot—are everlasting, deathless. For this reason, the arcade becomes Douglas's sanctuary from the losses of the summer—the deaths of Great-grandma and Colonel Freeleigh and the departure of John Huff. Before the season took its toll in human life, Douglas was a cocky little navigator in the stream of time. Afterward, he turns to the arcade for solace and escape as, at summer's end, his confidence in his alliance with time has been undermined. He philosophizes that everything there is to do in the arcade pays off. For every coin deposited in a slot there is action or reaction. Something always happens. The effect of this insight is like coming "forth in peace as from a church unknown before." Douglas's exuberant response to the mechanical amusements in the arcade is another example of enhancement at work. It is here that he discovers "Mme. Floristan Mariani Tarot, the Chiromancer, Soul Healer, and Deep-Down Diviner of Fates and Furies." If there is anything he consciously wants, it's someone who can heal his bereaved soul and read his uncertain fate. In the spirit of revelation, he believes that beneath Mme. Tarot's metal exterior and inside her machinery there is a captivating Italian girl, a princess under a spell, imprisoned in wax. When he deciphers the word *Secours* written, as he believes, in lemon juice under her "regular" message, he is sure she is a prisoner of Mr. Black, the proprietor.

With the help of Tom and his father, who can recall his own fascination with the circus, Douglas steals the Tarot Witch. He vows to master the arts of black magic and to free her from captivity. Then in gratitude she will foretell his future, save him from accidents, insure his immortality—in short, empower him to sing and dance in defiance of death. This episode is another example of how, for Bradbury's boys, belief is not a matter of appearances belying facts; rather, appearances do, indeed, betoken truth, albeit a truth different from that perceived by adults. For Douglas and others of his race, the key is the arcana they construe from their natural psychic awareness and from bits and pieces of occult lore combined with an ingenuous faith in supernatural agencies.

The large and small daily dramas of life revolve around Douglas, each one involving him differently, each touching him and leaving its illumination. The summer's changes and losses engender a written recitative in his journal, his personal "history of a dying world." He transcribes his testament by the wan and fitful light of the fireflies he has collected in a Mason jar for just this momentous entry in his record of revelations and discoveries. The eerie green glow or halflight emitted by the insects befits his grim denunciation:

YOU CAN'T DEPEND ON *THINGS* BECAUSE . . .
*. . . like machines, for instance, they fall apart
or rust or rot, or maybe never get finished at all . . .
or wind up in garages . . .*

*. . . like tennis shoes, you can only run so far,
so fast, and then the earth's got you again . . .*

*. . . like trolleys. Trolleys, big as they are,
always come to the end of the line . . .*

YOU CAN'T DEPEND ON *PEOPLE* BECAUSE . . .
*. . . they go away.
. . . strangers die.
. . . people you know fairly well die.
. . . friends die.
. . . people murder people, like in books.
. . . your own folks can die.*

In addition to revealing dejection over the end of human relationships, Douglas's statement reveals his disappointment when rare contraptions fail: Leo Auffmann's Happiness Machine, the Green Machine (the only electric car in town), and the retired trolley.

Until the summer's toll, Douglas typified the members of his race in believing that he was immortal. Now, unexpectedly, time and death have come to collect, and they must be reckoned with. The scene containing the foregoing passage shows Douglas an unresolved mixture of defiance and resignation. It also foreshadows his own near-fatal encounter with death. Abed in his room, he is swept into unconsciousness by a fever as "killing hot" as the August month. Powerless to cure him, his family can only pray for the languishing boy now lost in a limbo fraught with hallucinations and spectres. In desperation, Tom appeals to someone he knows will have the special cure for his brother: Mr. Jonas, the junkman. Mr. Jonas has a hoard of treasures in the guise of junk to swap or give away. As an all-around good Samaritan, he is also known to have remedies for affliction, to give people rides in his wagon, to deliver babies, to keep sleepless souls company till dawn. Bradbury suggests that he is unworldly, wise, and benevolent.

In response to Tom's appeal, the local sage diagnoses Douglas's ailment. Douglas, he claims, was born to suffer emotionally. He is one of those special people who "bruise easier, tire faster, cry quicker, remember longer." Without hesitation, Mr. Jonas concocts a miracle in the form of aromatic spirits of rare and wholesome air, vintage winds and breezes like "green dusk for dreaming," blended with assorted fruits and herbs, the various sweet plants of earth. Then without witnesses or fanfare and in the secrecy of deep night, he leaves his brew for Douglas to inhale, literally to inspire. Revived, restored, and returned to the land of the living, Douglas exhales the spellbinding breath of his redemption, a blend of "cool night and cool water and cool white snow and cool green moss, and moonlight on silver pebbles lying at the bottom of a quiet river and cool clear water at the bottom of a small white stone wall." Appropriately, both the solution that enables Douglas to survive the crisis of mortality and the person who administers it are extraordinary. The elixir and Mr. Jonas belong to a dimension where enchantment is the norm.

In "The Man Upstairs," a short story not part of the collection in *Dandelion Wine*, 11-year-old Douglas Spaulding single-handedly uncovers the incredible identity of "something not-human" that comes in the guise of a boarder to live with him in his grandparents' house. Immediately he instinctively dislikes the grim, black-garbed Mr. Koberman whose forbidding presence changes the very character of his room. Sensing something "alien and brittle," Douglas wonders about the stranger who works at night and sleeps by day, who uses his own wooden cutlery at meals, and who carries only new copper pennies in his pockets. One of Bradbury's most original devices becomes the means by which Douglas, with uncanny detection, reveals the "vampire" or "monster" presumably responsible for the "peculiar" deaths in town. On the landing between the first and second floors there is an "enchanted" stained-glass window where in the early mornings, Douglas stands "entranced," "peering at the world through multicolored windows." One morning he happens to see Mr. Koberman on his way home and Douglas is shocked by what he sees:

The glass *did* things to Mr. Koberman. His face, his suit, his hands. The clothes seemed to melt away. Douglas almost believed, for one terrible instant, that he could see *inside* Mr. Koberman. And what he saw made him lean wildly against the small red pane, blinking.

After Koberman deliberately breaks the magic window, Douglas turns the panes into instruments of revelation with a dexterity worthy of his grandmother's expertise with chickens. Watching grandmother, "a kindly, gentle-faced, white-haired old witch," clean and dress chickens is one of Douglas's "prime thrills" in life. His delight and curiosity during her regular preparation of the birds partly explains the inspiration for his imaginative, intrepid, and resourceful method of destroying the unnatural Koberman. Douglas's fascination is significant. There, amid "twenty knives in the various squeaking drawers of the magic kitchen table," he is absorbed as grandmother performs her art.

In this story, young Douglas, like his older version in *Dandelion Wine*, takes life head-on, fearing nothing. Like his grandmother, he calmly and adroitly vivisects Koberman. Inside the creature he discovers an assortment of strange objects of all shapes and sizes: a smelly bright orange elastic square with four blue tubes and a "bright pink linked chain with a purple triangle at one end." Everything he finds is pliable and resilient with the consistency of gelatin. When he sees that the monster is still alive after the operation, Douglas uses "six dollars and seventy cents worthy of silver dimes," the total amount in his bank, to kill him. Without hysteria or commotion—indeed, as though destroying something unnatural was the most natural act in the world—Douglas merely tells his grandfather that he has something to show him. "It's not nice, but it's interesting." To the adults, the Koberman episode is heinous—a "ghastly affair," according to Grandfather. Douglas, in contrast, is the willful innocent whose attraction to the inscrutable and aversion to the sinister stranger ordained his action. He can only wonder why it should be "bad" because he does not see or feel anything bad.

The authorities agree that Douglas's act was not murder but rather a "mercy." When Douglas speculates on the matter, he proudly appraises his handiwork and compares it to his grandmother's skill: "All in all, Mr. Koberman was as neat a job as any chicken ever popped into hell by Grandma." His complete lack of shock or terror recalls how his grandfather had teased him about being a "cold-blooded little pepper" and a "queer duck." Ironically, his composure is as unnatural from an adult point of view as his victim was to adults and children alike. Throughout the story Bradbury shows that Douglas is indisposed by Koberman's presence and habits, as well as intrigued and repelled by his strangeness. These factors, combined with his fascination with the ritual carnage in his grandmother's kitchen, prompt his self-styled liberties with life and death. In *Dandelion Wine* Douglas celebrates with radiant subjectivity the sanctity of life in nature and humanity; in "The Man Upstairs" he exhibits an unabashed objective preoccupation with living organisms and their vital processes, from the lowly chicken to a lowly subhuman grotesque. Any means justify his ends. That Koberman is a menace does not seem to be as imperative to him as the irrefutable fact of Koberman's difference, his essential alienness. Douglas's audacity and imperturbability are a strain of ruthlessness we find full-blown in the children Bradbury creates in "The Veldt," "The Small Assassin," and "Let's Play 'Poison'." The children of these three stories destroy adults who threaten their autonomy. In "The Man Upstairs" Douglas plays judge and executioner only secondarily, or incidentally, to satisfy his curiosity, eliminate a nuisance, and practice, as his grandmother's disciple, his version of fowl butchery.

If the Green Town that Douglas and Tom Spaulding inhabit is a latter-day Arcady—a summer idyll, even with the changes and losses of 1928—then the Green Town that James Nightshade and William Halloway inhabit is "October Country." The town of *Something Wicked This Way Comes* is singled out for a visit by a pair of underworlders who run a sinister circus out of season. Will's father recalls an old religious tract which explains the origins of Cooger and Dark and sets the tone for the events of the novel:

> "For these beings, fall is the ever normal season, the only weather, there be no choice beyond. Where do they come from? The dust. Where do they go? The grave. Does blood stir in their veins? No: the night wind. What ticks in their head? The worm. What speaks from their mouth? The toad. What sees from their eye? The snake. What hears with their ear? The abyss between the stars. They sift the human storm for souls, eat flesh of reason, fill tombs with sinners. They frenzy forth. In gusts they beetle-scurry, creep, thread, filter, motion, make all moons sullen, and surely cloud all clear-run waters. The spider-web hears them, trembles—breaks. Such are the autumn people. Beware of them."

To underscore this motif, Bradbury has created as his principal characters two boys who are native to the season, born two minutes apart on Halloween. Their names—Halloway and especially Nightshade—are thematically meaningful. Close by nativity, next-door neighbors, and best friends, they are, nevertheless, a study in contrasts. Will is "one human all good," the offspring of a "man half-bad and a woman half-bad" who "put their good halves together." His surname serves as a characternym: Halloway. He goes a *hallowed* way. Will is trusting and sunny. The elder Halloway ponders the difference between his son and Jim, and marks Will's innocence:

> . . . he's the last peach, high on a summer tree. Some boys walk by and you cry, seeing them. They feel good, they are good . . . you know, seeing them pass, that's how they'll be all their life; they'll get hit, hurt, cut, bruised, and always wonder why, why does it happen? how can it happen to *them?*

Jim Nightshade, in contrast, is intense, enigmatic, and high-powered. A natural scamp, he is always ready for adventure, particularly under cover of darkness. Bradbury declares that "no one else in the world had a name came so well off the tongue." Indeed, an intensity and quality of darkness consonant with his surname pervade his visage and temperament. Charles Halloway wonders:

> Why are some people grasshopper fiddlings, scrapings, all antennae shivering, one big ganglion eternally knotting, slip-knotting, square-knotting themselves? They stoke a furnace all their lives, sweat their lips, shine their eyes and start it all in the crib. Caesar's lean and hungry friends. They eat the dark, who only stand and breathe.
> That's Jim, all bramblehair and itchweed.

Jim is the perpetual and spirited seeker who, around his widowed mother, is absent-spirited and reserved. Everywhere he gives off a steely resolve to outrace time. Similar to Joe Pipkin in *The Halloween Tree* and John Huff in *Dandelion Wine*, Jim is descended from Mercury. His feet are winged, and running is his natural means of locomotion. Enchantment is his psychic milieu. Compelled by a smoldering passion for experience, he is reminiscent of Hermann Hesse's Demian: "as primeval, animal, marble, beautiful and cold . . . secretly filled with fabulous life." In his isolation and independence, Jim ranges the town like a demon—not exactly supernatural but elusive and a shade more than human; he is intermediate between the extra-human and the human. "Marbled with dark," Jim is "the kite, the wild twine cut . . . as high and dark and suddenly strange." Better than anyone else, Will understands their differences:

> And running, Will thought, Boy, it's the same old thing. I talk. Jim runs. I tilt stones, Jim grabs the cold junk under the

stones and—lickety-split! I climb hills, Jim yells off church steeples. I got a bank account, Jim's got the hair on his head, the yell in his mouth, the shirt on his back and the tennis shoes on his feet. How come I think he's richer? Because, Will thought, I sit on a rock in the sun and old Jim, he prickles his armhairs by moonlight and dances with hoptoads. I tend cows. Jim tames Gila monsters. Fool! I yell at Jim. Coward! he yells back.

Although they are as different as night and day, together Will and Jim form an invincible yet vulnerable brotherhood. They combine bright simplicity and dark complexity. Living within the sanctioned circle of home and the larger sphere of the town, they conspire to venture beyond the narrow world of adults. To resist enslavement to an orderly, predictable existence, they cavort on the outskirts of Green Town where Rolfe's Moon Meadow becomes the wilderness equivalent of the ravine in *Dandelion Wine*. In contrast to the group in *Dandelion Wine* and the larger tribe of nine in *The Halloween Tree*, there are only two representatives of Bradbury's separate race in *Something Wicked This Way Comes*. The curious cult formed by the two boys in *Something Wicked* is all the more dramatic for its polarities, which heighten the efficacy of their bond. Will and Jim join the tender and the firm, the bold and the gentle.

The pursuits and pastimes of this doughty pair usually occur under the protection of the moon, when they "softly printed the night with treads," like creatures liberated and afoot when most human beings sleep. Brothers of nocturnal creatures similar to the wind, "they felt wings on their fingers" and "plunged in new sweeps of air" to fly to their destination. All of Bradbury's boys are glorious runners; in spirit they are a cross between bird and man.

To observe their rites and ceremonies, Will and Jim use private signals and symbols. They "prefer to chunk dirt at clapboards, hurl acorns down roof shingles, or leave mysterious notes flapping from kites stranded on attic window sills." Their most elaborate strategy derives from a relic pine-plank boardwalk that Will's grandfather preserved in the alley between the houses. The boys have contrived to make it into a transmitter, a crude but ingenious and serviceable apparatus on which one or the other summons his partner to leave his bedroom and descend the iron rungs embedded in the house and hidden by the ivy. "Ulmers" and "goffs" are examples of another way Will and Jim communicate. These are code words for the ugly, evil creatures that invade their sleep, souring dreams into nightmares.

The only place in Green Town that can match their double-duty imagination is the library where Charles Halloway works. For the boys it is "a factory of spices from far countries," fabulous with accounts of both real and fictitious events to transport them from the ordinary to the extraordinary. Yet nothing heroic or cataclysmic recorded in books can match the dreadful events that befall Will and Jim when Cooger and Dark's Pandemonium Shadow Show comes like a plague to town. Well named, the carnival of devastation is operated by two immortal hellhounds who have been wreaking their horrors every twenty to forty years for at least a hundred years.

On an ominous night in October the theater of evil arrives, heralded by a poster-hanger plaintively singing a Christmas carol. The "terrified elation" of Charles Halloway portends the doom bearing down on him, his son, Jim, Miss Foley the teacher, Mr. Crosetti the barber, and other unwary residents. Bradbury chooses the "special hour" of 3:00 A.M. when "the soul is out" and it is "a long way back to sunset, a far way on to dawn" for the coming of the circus train. It pulls into Rolfe's Moon Meadow to the infernal wail of a play-erless calliope which sounds like church music unnervingly changed.

Will and Jim respond to the train whistle, summoning thoughts of the "grieving sounds" that all trains make in the deep of night. Accompanied by fluttering black pennants and black confetti, the carnival's whistle is more poignant than any the boys had ever heard. Bradbury uses enchantment to catch the boys' attitude toward the whistle that sounds like "the wails of a lifetime," "the howl of moon-dreamed dogs," "a thousand fire sirens weeping, or worse." The calamitous sound is so excruciating that Will and Jim shriek and scream, lurch and writhe in involuntary concert with the lament, like "groans of a billion people dead or dying."

Pursuing the sound, they watch as Mr. Dark, another of Bradbury's illustrated characters, emerges "all dark suit, shadow-faced" and gestures the train to life. The awed witnesses hardly dare to believe their eyes, but at the same time they are too engrossed to doubt what they behold. From its unnat-ural beginnings, Will and Jim know that what has come to town is no ordi-nary circus. When the tents materialize from fragments of the night sky and not canvas, they know the circus is worse than strange; it is wrong.

The hell on wheels that passes for a circus will test the boys' innocence, their "patterns of grace," with diabolical amusements and attractions. One is the fatal Mirror Maze, "like winter standing tall, waiting to kill you with a glance." Another is the "lunatic carousel" that runs backwards, unwinding the years, or forward, whirling them ahead, to leave the rider changed in size, but unchanged inside, either too young or too old in body for a brain that stood still. To their horror, Will and Jim find that the seller of lightening rods, who at the beginning of the story sells Jim an elaborate model, has been transformed by Cooger and Dark into a dwarf, "his eyes like broken splin-ters of brown marble now bright-on-the-surface, now deeply mournfully forever-lost-and-gone-buried-away mad."

The carnival thrives on human sensuality, vanities, cravings, fantasies, and nightmares. Bradbury intimates that the boys' salvation derives from their attributes as members of his separate race. The ordeal they undergo in resisting the perverse attractions of the Shadow Show proves their fortuity as innocents. Unlike the adults who succumb, they withstand the atrocious marvels of the carnival and survive the vengeance of Mr. Dark. The depraved Cooger and Dark are dealers in phantasms. As agents of Satan, they range the world to ensnare and afflict the souls of the weak and gullible. With Charles Halloway as his spokesman, Bradbury explains that Cooger and Dark are monsters who have "learned to live off souls." People, he conjectures, "jump at the chance to give up everything for nothing." Souls are, above all, free for the taking, because most people do not understand or appreciate what they give away "slapstick" until it is lost.

The side-show freaks were all "sinners who've taken on the shape of their original sins." They have been damned to live as physical representatives of the sins they practiced before encountering Cooger and Dark. Tortured by guilty consciences, they are "madmen waiting to be released from bondage, meantime servicing the carnival, giving it coke for its ovens." The cast of grotesques and list of their transgressions outnumber the Seven Deadly Sins. In contrast to these poor wretches, Will and Jim possess certain natural virtues, chiefly justice and fortitude, as well as three theological virtues—faith, hope, and charity. Even so, everyone has it in him or her, Halloway cautions, to be an autumn person. Children like Will and Jim are still summer people, "rare" and "fine."

Here, as in *Dandelion Wine*, Bradbury delineates children's relationship with time. In *Something Wicked This Way Comes* he enlarges and distorts the symbols that stand for the preoccupations of adults. One is the mirror with which they worship appearances, while another is chance, or fortune, which they court as Lady Luck. Allegorically, the carnival shows how such instruments and behavior can warp their lives and lead them to perdition. In the story adults who rely on appearances and who gamble with destiny are lured by the Mirror Maze, the Dust Witch, and the wayward carousel. All are distorted expressions of human superficiality and frivolity. As members of the race of children, Will and Jim are neither victims of vanity nor fatalists. Gamboling apace of time, they are not slowed by dependence on the past nor driven by pursuit of the future. Unlike the acts and amusements of the carnival, their games and escapades are harmless. They escape from Cooger and Dark because they are integral personalities. They are innocent because they are free of sin, and this is their ultimate protection.

In Bradbury's modern variation on a morality play, Cooger and Dark perpetrate a studiously false fantasy world, grotesque and lethal. Timeless villains, they represent time deranged. But their ministry of evil is challenged by two boys whose spontaneous whim-wham and sportive spirits overcome their machinations. As Charles Halloway says, "sometimes good has weapons and evil none." He can only stand back and marvel at the boys, in loving envy of their characteristics as a breed. He knows very well that while he can advise them, he cannot share their camaraderie and freedom.

Chapters 29 and 30 are a surprising switch. Until then, one senses that Jim is the leader, the one who initiates action, the real daredevil of the two. Indeed, he does hear "ticks from clocks" that tell "another time"; but it is Will whose courage and inventiveness foil the Dust Witch sent by Dark to find out where the boys live. When her balloon approaches, they know that

> She could dip down her hands to feel the bumps of the world, touch house roofs, probe attic bins, reap dust, examine draughts that blew through halls and souls that blew through people, draughts vented from bellows to thump-wrist, to pound-temples, to pulse-throat, and back to bellows again.

Although scared, Will plays his hunch and jumps lively. He uses the garden hose to wash away the "silver-slick" ribbon the Dust Witch paints on the roof of Jim's house to mark it for easy detection when Dark comes to capture them. But that is only a partial solution, for Will knows that the witch is still aloft, ready to return to the meadow and report to Dark. Armed with his Boy Scout bow and arrows, he challenges the witch to a kind of match. His plan is to lure her to an empty house and there, atop its roof, shoot her balloon with an arrow and puncture it. But his bow breaks before he can discharge an arrow. Undaunted, he throws the arrowhead at the balloon and slits the surface of the "gigantic pear" as "dungeon air raved out, as dragon breath gushed forth." Alone, Will defeats the Dust Witch, though he nearly breaks his neck in the process.

The determination and defiance that Will exhibits in this episode pave the way for the desperate antics of he and his father when Jim's life is at stake. Believing Jim dead, Will bursts into tears, only to be urged by his father to vent another kind of hysteria—the madness and hilarity of absolute defiance:

> "... Damn it, Willy, all this, all these, Mr. Dark and his sort, they *like* crying, my God, they *love* tears! Jesus God, the more you bawl, the more they drink the salt off your chin. Wail and they suck your breath like cats. Get up! Get off your knees, damn it! Jump around! Whoop and holler! You hear! Shout, Will, sing, but most of all laugh, you got that, laugh!"

Will and his father resurrect Jim with levity, not gravity—with mirth, not lamentation. Their rhapsody and bombast—indeed, their grandiosity—is Dionysian: redemption in revelry.

Like Douglas Spaulding's cure, Jim Nightshade's revival is miraculous. Cooger and Dark are destroyed and their captive freaks are liberated. The boys emerge from the meadow unscathed. They are "exultant" as they leave the wilderness behind. Together with Charles Halloway, they bang "a trio of shouts down the wind."

In "Jack-in-the-Box" and "The Veldt," Bradbury has created two technologically advanced houses which are the center of life for several of his young characters. In the first story, Edwin's explorations take place in a vast house designed as a substitute for the natural world. Unlike the wilderness of the ravine in *Dandelion Wine* and the meadow in *Something Wicked This Way Comes*, the interior geography of "Jack-in-the-Box" is precisely circumscribed and carefully controlled. What's more, Edwin's access to the various regions is rigidly prescribed. On each birthday he is allowed to enter another part of the house. The second story has a house equipped with a psychoramic playroom. There Wendy and Peter Hadley can range anywhere in the world. Dominance of one species by another is an important aspect of both stories. In "Jack-in-the-Box," adults are the overlords until the end, whereas, in "The Veldt," the Hadley parents abdicate their authority to the superhouse which, in cahoots with their children, conspires to win complete dominance.

The only world Edwin has ever known is the multistoried domain built by his late father as a self-sufficient hideaway and bulwark against the world at large. Perhaps more than any other child in Bradbury's fiction, Edwin is an innocent incarcerated by adult neuroses, subjugated by the delusions and defenses erected as compensation by adults in retreat from life. Like his toy, the jack-in-the-box, he is confined, even trapped.

His dying mother (who, unbeknown to him, doubles as his teacher) has nurtured him on the legend of a godlike father destroyed by society, whose legacy is the universe of the house, safely cloistered in a wilderness tract beyond the deadly clutches of the "Beasts." He is taught that a circumscribed existence in the house means life and happiness but that death awaits him beyond the dense circle of trees which make the estate an enclave. His indoctrination makes everything—most of all, himself—fit into place:

> Here, in the Highlands, to the soft sound of Teacher's voice running on, Edwin learned what was expected of him and his body. He was to grow into a Presence, he must fit the odors and the trumpet voice of God. He must some day stand tall and burning with pale fire at this high window to shout dust off the beams of the Worlds; he must be God Himself! Nothing must prevent it. Not the sky or the trees or the Things beyond the trees.

We learn from his mother's cryptic remarks that Edwin's father was killed (before Edwin's birth)—"struck down by one of those Terrors on the road." Her attitude and admonitions are thinly veiled denunciations of the way human beings have turned their machines, chiefly automobiles, into weapons of destruction.

In describing Edwin, Bradbury creates the image of a lonely, delicate boy. Like his mother, Edwin is otherworldly. Pensive and luminous, he is an *isolato* who wanders among the artificial climates of the house:

> And her child, Edwin, was the thistle that one breath of wind might unpod in a season of thistles. His hair was silken and his eyes were of a constant blue and feverish temperature. He had a haunted look, as if he slept poorly. He might fly apart like a packet of ladyfinger firecrackers if a certain door slammed.

His isolation from others of his race, however, has not repressed or weakened the attributes he shares with boys like Douglas Spaulding and Jim Nightshade. Shut in though he is, he is a latent leaper and runner whose agitation is a prelude to flight and reason. Not even the persistent legend of his mighty father and the house that will someday be his kingdom can quell his curiosity about the outside. When he longs to see the Beasts, we know that his mother's systematic attempts to inculcate a fear of society have failed. The house, too, has failed, for Edwin's unrest implies that a child's mind and emotions thrive when, unrestrained, he is free to grow where his imagination and feet lead him. Edwin's curiosity also suggests that the seemingly ideal setting created by adults is inadequate. In creating their own playgrounds, children are architects whose imaginary constructs and original renovations do not need to conform to conventions and rules.

On the day when Edwin finds his mother dead, he flees from the house and garden world to run jubilantly among the "Terrors" and "Beasts" of town, touching everything he can reach, filling his eyes and mind with life. In a world wondrously new to him, he is finally free, like the jack-in-the-box he liberates by throwing it out of the house. Joining his counterparts in Bradbury's other stories, Edwin exults in the flux of time, awash in its tides, reborn on its crest.

"The Veldt," "The Small Assassin," and "Let's Play 'Poison'" are a trio of stories with diabolical children. Together, they comprise a fiendish tribe within the separate race. In "The Veldt," Bradbury takes up the theme of the insidious struggle for total power and control that children wage behind the facade of innocence. Though only ten years old, Wendy and Peter Hadley know that their parents are a mortal threat to the real and imaginary geographies which they can project in their electronically cosmic nursery. When George and Lydia Hadley begin to worry about their children's obsession with a particular setting, George insists that they have nothing to fear from a purely mechanical wonder that is "dimensional superreactionary, supersensitive color film and mental tape film behind glass screens." His sophisticated terminology, however, does not explain the children's keen interest in the recurring veldt scene. The children's psychological alienation has produced the reality of Africa. Each time they project their wishes, the veldt materializes with greater intensity, until it is fully animated and empowered to serve their ends.

The Hadley's Happylife Home—the complete home of the future— has usurped their role. Supremely attentive to all the needs of the children and their parents, the house has advanced technological means for disaffecting the children. The playroom, in particular, has succeeded in its takeover by systematically fulfilling their fantasies. In its role as surrogate, it provides a reliable escape to exotic lands for Wendy and Peter. But the African projection stops being child's play when it becomes a daily rehearsal for parental carnage.

The correspondence between the names of James Barrie's memorable characters in *Peter Pan* and those of Bradbury's children cannot be coincidental. In both works of fiction, Wendy and Peter are devotees of never-never land, a dimension that is beyond the constraints and conventions imposed on demanding, if not persecuting, adults, and which is outside the limitations and changes decreed by time. In "The Veldt," Wendy and Peter go beyond the point of no return. The vengeance they wreak on their parents leaves them unaffected and undisturbed. Afterward, when David McClean, a psychologist and family friend, finds them nonchalantly and cheerfully picnicking in the savage setting they have stimulated, they show no signs of remorse or guilt. They are unholy terrors for whom expediency and self-preservation are the sole dictates of behavior. Like the baby in the next story, they are amoral and conscience-free.

The unnamed infant in "The Small Assassin" is the most precocious terror of the lot. Even before his birth his mother has undeniable intimations of his deadly intentions. Vainly, Alice Leiber tries to tell David, his father, how "vulnerable" they are to him, because "it's too young to know love, or a law of love . . . so new, so amoral, so conscience-free." With cunning treachery the baby murders Alice and later, David. After Alice's death, David theorizes about the unconscionable cause and effect. He maintains that the infant is motivated by hate for being expelled from his mother's womb into a precarious existence at the mercy of adults. He sees the baby as only one of possibly countless infant aliens—"strange, red little creatures with brains that work in a bloody darkness we can't even guess at." David argues that they have "elemental little brains, aswarm with racial memory, hatred, and raw cruelty, with no more thought than self-preservation." His speculations force him to conclude that his son is a freak, preternaturally "born perfectly aware, able to think, instinctively." Like insects and animals, he was at birth capable of certain functions which normally develop gradually:

> "Wouldn't it be a perfect setup, a perfect blind for anything the baby might want to do? He could pretend to be ordinary, weak, crying, ignorant. With just a *little* expenditure of energy he could crawl about a darkened house, listening. And how easy to place obstacles at the top of stairs. How easy to cry all night and tire a mother into pneumonia. How easy, right at birth, to be so close to the mother that *a few deft maneuvers might cause peritonitis!*"

The family doctor, who is a staunch advocate of a "thousand years of accepted medical belief," persists in believing that the child is "helpless, not responsible." Not until the infant turns on the gas in his father's room and asphyxiates him does the horrified Dr. Jeffers admit that the Leiber baby is an unnatural, scheming menace who must be stopped. In extrapolating the infant's motivation from reasonable psychological theory, Bradbury conjectures that all children have the potential for Baby Leiber's destructive *élan vital.*

In the last story of this unsettling trio, Bradbury depicts children per se as antagonists. In the opening scene sixteen children maliciously and capriciously send one of their classmates to his death from a third-floor window. Mr. Howard, their teacher, is appalled, and resigns after suffering a nervous breakdown. It is he who most clearly articulates Bradbury's position: "Sometimes, I actually believe that children are invaders from another dimension." The authorities dismiss the event as an accident, contending that the children could not have understood what they did. Howard, made irascible if not paranoid by the tragedy, disputes this. He believes he knows the terrible truth:

> ". . . sometimes I believe children are little monsters thrust out of hell, because the devil could no longer cope with them. And I certainly believe that everything should be done to reform their uncivil little minds. . . .
>
> "You are another race entirely, your motives, your beliefs, your disobediences. . . . You are not human. You are—children."

To Howard's way of thinking, all children belong to a cult of aliens. Subterfuge and subversion are their natural modus operandi. Their choice of playgrounds is sufficient evidence, for they love "excavations, hiding-places, pipes, and conduits and trenches." If Howard knew the Spaulding brothers and the other boys in *Dandelion Wine,* he would acknowledge with considerable horror but no surprise that their favorite haunt, the ravine, is a no-man's land fit only for subhuman creatures. Certainly he would count Jim Nightshade and Will Halloway among the race of little aliens, because they love to reconnoiter at night. Howard decided that even children's games are too fiendish. Hopscotch, for example, is hardly what it seems to adults. The figures drawn on the ground are actually pentagrams. Other sports are accompanied not by innocent rhymes but by incantations disguised by sometimes sweet yet often taunting voices.

The morbid game through which Howard is perversely immortalized is called "Poison." His introduction to this pastime with its dead men, graves, and poison—only confirms his convictions about children. His dread of children inspires dread in the children who know him. The animosity is reciprocal. The mischief they cause in retaliation to his outbursts and attacks is inevitable, and vice versa. The open conflict precipitates Howard's doom when, in pursuit of his tormentors, he falls into an excavation and is buried alive. The cement square that later covers the spot bears the not-so-accidental inscription: "M. Howard—R.I.P." Alive, he was the adversary of a race whose members were his nemesis. Dead, he is profaned whenever they dance on his makeshift grave as they play "Poison."

As a separate race, Bradbury's children are uninhibited earthly creatures with an unalloyed, undiluted exuberance. Their innocence enables them to transcend the forces that influence and often control the lives of adults. In his fiction, children live and move in a dimension where they are generally exempt from the dilemmas that afflict their elders. Each sphere of activity—home, town, wilderness—has heightened or enhanced elements which, to them, give it a psychological credence that it does not possess for the adults with whom they share it.

Unlike their parents, Bradbury's children are not hounded by time. All things considered, it's as though they course in tune with time in all its seasons. Unthreatened by a sense of mutability and mortality, they have a capacity for unequivocal, immediate action that is neither complicated nor diminished by the second thoughts which lead adults to prudence, apprehension, or indecision. The impulsive spontaneous behavior of Bradbury's boys is seldom spoiled by conscience, for egocentricity is their prime mover.

The adults they treat with disdain are people whose authenticity they doubt. The adults they respect are individuals whose lives they can romanticize and enter with vicarious abandon. For some of Bradbury's children, however, all adults are adversaries simply because they belong to another race—separate and different if only for an age. Engrossed in their own exploits or engaged in a conflict with adults to preserve their ethos, the children who inhabit Bradbury's stories might well exclaim with e. e. cummings: "we're anything brighter than even the sun."

GARY K. WOLFE

The Frontier Myth in Ray Bradbury

In an interview in 1961 Ray Bradbury described an unwritten story of his which was to be cast in the form of an American Indian legend. An old Indian tells of a trip he made years earlier to visit tribes in the East. During this trip a strange event occurs: "One night there was a smell on the wind, there was a sound coming from a great distance." Nature seems suddenly transformed and silent, as though a great event is about to take place. Searching for the source of this portent, the Indian and his young grandson wander for days, finally coming to the edge of the sea and spotting a campfire in the distance. Beyond, in the water, are anchored three ships. Creeping closer, the Indians find that the fire is surrounded by strange-looking men who speak an unknown language, who "have huge sort of metal devices on their heads," and carry strange mechanical weapons. The Indians return to the wilderness, vaguely aware that some great event has happened and that the wilderness will never be the same, but not at all sure what the event is or exactly what it means.

This small unwritten fable of the coming of the first Europeans to North America is significant not only because parts of it appear in another context in the story "Ylla" in *The Martian Chronicles* (once selected by Bradbury as his favorite among his stories)—in which the Indians become Martians and the strange sense of foreboding becomes telepathy—but also

From *Ray Bradbury*. © 1980 by Martin Harry Greenberg and Joseph D. Olander.

for the way in which the story reveals a romantic, almost mystical, vision of historical experience, particularly the experience of the American wilderness. Somehow the wilderness is transformed by the mere presence of the newcomers even before there has been any interaction between them and the Indians. A similar vision if generated early in *The Martian Chronicles*. The Martians sense that "something terrible will happen in the morning" before they are aware of the coming of the Earthmen. The similarity is hardly accidental; Bradbury goes on to comment about this Indian fable: "Well, this is a science fiction story, really, isn't it? What have we seen here? . . . these scientists set out their three ships as our rocket people will set out for far planets in the near future and discover new worlds with these devices which represent mankind's desire to know more, to go against ignorance, to dare nature, to risk annihilation and to gather knowledge." In other words, science fiction need not take place on distant planets or in the far future; all it needs to do is portray a quest for knowledge that is in some way aided by technological devices.

In the same interview Bradbury describes another Indian story which was to have taken place centuries later, when Plains Indians "hear a great sound like the thundering herd from a distance and see coming across the plains at night the first locomotive and this thing throwing fire, the great dragon. How terrifying a sight this must have been." This story also appeared in a different setting, as "The Dragon" in *A Medicine for Melancholy*, but with the Indians replaced not by Martians but by medieval English knights who encounter a locomotive through some sort of time warp.

Both unwritten Indian stories demonstrate how Bradbury's imagination is drawn to speculate on significant moments in history, as well as the impact of specific technologies on these moments. In both cases, the published stories, using similar ideas, disguise their quasi-historical origin by transmuting the action into fantasies of space and time. Although these examples are probably atypical of Bradbury's interest in history (it isn't likely that many of his stories began as pseudo-Indian legends), it has been widely noted that Bradbury's most famous work, *The Martian Chronicles*, "talks about the colonization of Mars in terms of the colonization of America," and is, in fact, a view of history thinly disguised as science fiction.

Bradbury's comment that his Indian legend is actually science fiction is further evidence of this. To Bradbury, science fiction is not the progress of science projected into alternate worlds, but rather fiction dealing with the impact of various forms of technology on societies that are familiar to the reader. This focus is not, of course, unique to Bradbury; Bradbury merely provides what may be one of the clearest links between the traditional frontier orientation of much of American literature and the attempts to extend this orientation into new worlds, which is characteristic of a great deal of science fiction. Although often dismissed from the mainstream of science fiction for his "anti-science" attitudes, Bradbury, in fact, shares with most of the science fiction that preceded him an interest in *technology*, as opposed to *science*. As Lewis Mumford and others have often pointed out, the impact of technology is best explored through historical, rather than scientific, paradigms. There is little science in Bradbury, but there are lots of machines, machines which are seen in terms of what they do to the progress of society, not the progress of knowledge.

This concept of technology, as providing a social frontier, is an old one in science fiction, familiar even to nonreaders from the famous "Star Trek" motto, "Space—the final frontier." Indeed, it is not unreasonable to speculate that the surge in popularity of science fiction in the last century may be partly attributed not only to the increasing impact of technology on daily life but also to the closing of the available frontiers which had provided settings for much adventure fiction until that time. The closing of the American frontier with the 1890 census—in the view of Frederick Jackson Turner, a symbolic event in the development of American democracy—was accompanied by a shift in frontier fiction from the Cooperesque vision of the frontier as meeting place between nature and civilization to what John Cawelti calls an "open society" with few laws and much violence, in many ways, not unlike the urban milieu of gangster fiction. In the decades that followed, the frontier experience of the great imperialist nations such as England was increasingly curtailed by moves toward independence and self-government in Africa, Asia, and South America. As explorers moved steadily into the hitherto unknown regions of Africa, the Arctic, and the Antarctic, the dreams of lost worlds that had characterized the fiction of Haggard and others began to fade.

Science fiction emerged, at least in part, as a way of retaining some sort of frontier experience. Though the genre's response to the need for new social frontiers was complex, it is possible to discern three major paradigms of frontier experience that have characterized much of this kind of science fiction since the turn of the century. First is the simple adventure story typified by the writing of Edgar Rice Burroughs, whose alien settings seem designed to do little more than give his heroic protagonists a new environment in which to demonstrate their natural superiority, thus offering further "proof" of the Cooperesque notion of a natural aristocracy that emerges clearly only in wilderness or savage environments. It is probably no accident that Burroughs also wrote Westerns or that John Carter's first adventure on Mars begins in Arizona in 1866, with Carter trapped by Indians. But Burroughs' Mars is for heroes, not settlers. It would be as unthinkable for

Earthmen to colonize "Barsoom" in his books as it would be for Tarzan to sell real estate.

Another paradigm, one that dominated science fiction in the forties and fifties, views the colonization of other worlds as an inevitable next step in the expansion of contemporary society. This is evident in the titles of anthologies from the period: *Beachheads in Space* (August Derleth, 1952); *The Space Frontiers* (Roger Lee Vernon, 1955); *Tomorrow, the Stars* (Robert Heinlein, 1952); *Frontiers in Space* (Bleiler and Dikty, 1955); and so on. It was from stories of this period, particularly Asimov's *Foundation* trilogy, that Donald Wollheim evolved his hypothetical "consensus cosmology," which he regards as underlying nearly all modern science fiction, and which portrays the human race as not only achieving interplanetary and interstellar travel and establishing a galactic empire, but as ultimately coming face to face with God himself in a final challenge for dominion over the cosmos. But the tradition goes back much further. In Garrett P. Serviss's *Edison's Conquest of Mars* (1898), for example, the portrayal of real scientists such as Edison, Kelvin, and Moissan as bizarre hybrids of Tom Swift and Daniel Boone makes clear the transformation of the frontier hero into the scientific hero.

The third paradigm, one that is somewhat more complex then the others, tends to be critical of the search for new frontiers, suggesting instead that the energy devoted to conquering new worlds might be better spent in improving social conditions in the present one. Among these works are the numerous tales in which man is excluded from the galactic community or is repelled by an alien society because of his history of violence and war. Arthur C. Clarke, in both *Childhood's End* and *The City and the Stars*, depicts situations in which man is deemed too immature for expansion to other worlds. Even in the science-fiction films of the 1950s, a common theme is that man simply is not wanted—as the angry Martians warn after chasing away the would-be explorers in *Angry Red Planet* (1960) with a zoo of red-filtered monsters: "Do not come back." This theme can be traced to the works of H. G. Wells, who Selenites repel the Earthmen in *First Men in the Moon* and those inhabitants of "The Country of the Blind" quickly put to rest the dreams of glory of a sighted man who would be king. The most powerful critique of technological imperialism, though, is Wells' *The War of the Worlds*, in which the conquest of a frontier is portrayed from the victim's point of view. "What are these Martians?" asks the Curate, to which the narrator responds: "What are we?"

Bradbury's concept of the frontier draws from all three paradigms. Like Burroughs, he uses an imaginary Mars as a convenient landscape in which to work out his essentially Earthbound fictions. He isn't concerned very much about how his characters get there, and even less that his version of Mars should bear any relationship to scientific data other than the then-popular belief in canals and red deserts. Like Asimov and Wollheim, he views man's future progress and emigration to other worlds as inevitable, if not necessarily beneficial. And like Wells, he is critical of progress, concerned that social values may be lost in the face of technological expansion. In the Martian stories technology may succeed in liberating man from an unpromising environment, as it does in "Way in the Middle of the Air"; but at the same time it results in new environments just as destructive if not more so, for example, the totalitarian society of book-burners and the final atomic war. As a thirteen-year-old, Bradbury visited the 1933 World's Fair in Chicago. The motto of the fair—"Science Explores: Technology Executes: Man Conforms"—expresses in chilling terms what was to become a central fear of Bradbury's. For him, the technological frontier is a paradox: we cannot enjoy its benefits without also encountering its hazards. If a machine can take us to Mars, another can destroy us on Earth. This theme is evident in Bradbury's non-Martian stories. "The Veldt" shows us how an elaborate electronic nursery can become an instrument of murder, while "The Sound of Thunder" is about a time machine that endangers the present.

To see how technology affects the imaginary frontier of the Martian stories, we should first look at the two opposing aspects of the frontier that technology brings together: the landscape and the settlers. The frontier landscape, of course, is the surface of Mars, a deliberately poetic dreamworld of wine trees, golden fruits, crystal pillars, and harp books—images that are thrown at us without the slightest explanation to make them congruent to our own experience, and which thus attain a power comparable to that of equally fanciful visions of the New World, and later of California, characteristic of earlier frontier movements. But this wholly imaginary landscape is in sharp contrast to the settlers who invade it.

In establishing the clearest possible opposition between his immigrant-settlers and the landscape, Bradbury drew upon the most domestic and mundane images he had access to: his own Midwestern childhood. This aspect of *The Martian Chronicles* has probably drawn the most criticism from science fiction readers, who often complain that Bradbury's Martian colonies are simply transplanted Midwestern towns from the 1920s, that the characters are not believable inhabitants of the last decade of this century or the first decade of the next. But the future is not what the book is about. If we regard *The Martian Chronicles* as a kind of "thought experiment" to examine middle-class values, many of the apparent inconsistencies are resolved. What would happen if the American middle class of the first half of this century were suddenly given, through some mechanical means, access to an entirely new frontier for settlement? How would they repeat the experience of earlier frontiers, and how would they be different? That Bradbury was very much aware of the childhood sources of his "future" colonists is apparent in his interviews and essays. As early as 1950 he was explaining that "Mars is a mirror, not a crystal." "And so, taking the people from my home town, Waukegan, Illinois, my aunts and uncles and cousins who had been raised in a green land, I parceled them into rockets and sent them off to Mars. . . . I decided that my book would not be a looking crystal into the future, but simply a mirror in which each human Earthman would find his own image reflected." In 1960 he wrote, "I find whole families of people from 1928 showing up in the year 2000 and helping to colonize Mars."

With an opposition thus clearly established between the nostalgic reality of the small-town Midwest and the poetic fantasy of an alien Mars, Bradbury is left only with finding a convenient way to bring them together. The means he chooses is technology, which is partly why we are tempted to regard the book as science fiction, even though Bradbury spends no more time making his machines believable than he does making Mars astronomically accurate. But the machines are not intended to make the work more "scientific" or lend verisimilitude to the fantasy. Rather, they are intended to provide both a thematic and a literal bridge between the worlds of the Midwest and Mars. If Mars is a world of dream and the settlers are figures of memory, the machines represent a stage of cognition somewhere between the two. They are at once familiar and alien, familiar from boyhood fantasies, yet alien when placed in a society of real people. By and large, they are not technical marvels but social conveniences. Bradbury's rockets deliver mail and carry immigrants; his robots preserve the family unit ("The Long Years" and "I Sing the Body Electric!") or carry out childish fantasies ("Usher II" and "The Veldt").

Bradbury's concern with the social impact of such machines is nowhere more apparent than in the 1961 Cunningham interview:

> Now from the time of Napoleon to our time three inventions alone have made a big difference. The invention of the telegraph made it possible to send messages instantaneously back and forth over countries so that people could know the condition of their army and bring reinforcements. The invention of the locomotive and railroads—we were able then to transport men much more quickly and sometimes save the day and change the history of a particular country; and then number three, the invention of the machine gun at the end of, I believe, the Civil War, occurred, made it possible for one man to destroy a small army.

Bradbury goes on to comment on what he regards as the two major inventions of this century—the automobile and the atomic bomb. The atomic bomb, he believed in 1960, reduced the risk of a major war and helped make the United Nations a success, while the automobile changed our social patterns and stimulated the migratory instincts of Americans.

Apart from the curious militaristic bias displayed by Bradbury in these quotations, what is significant is the *kind* of machines he singles out. There is no mention of machines that directly aided agriculture or industry such as reapers and cotton gins. In fact, with the possible exception of the atomic bomb, all the machines Bradbury cites are in some way associated with the conquest and settlement of frontier areas. The telegraph established communication between settled and unsettled areas; the locomotive made rapid settlement of the frontier a reality; the machine gun made it easier to overcome local resistance; the automobile gave the individual freedom to move farther from the central community (although I am not necessarily suggesting that suburbia is the modern frontier!). In *The Martian Chronicles* there is even a role for the atomic bomb in the settlement of a new frontier. It seems clear that Bradbury's attitude toward technology is founded in the tradition of measuring the usefulness of machines according to how much they contribute to the rapid expansion of society in new areas.

Three machines dominate frontier life in *The Martian Chronicles*. The atomic bomb not only threatens the destruction of the old order but underlies the growing pattern of dehumanization and paranoia that drives many settlers to Mars. The rocket serves, consecutively, the role of the explorers' ship and the railroad, first bringing the three reconnaissance expeditions to Mars and later bringing in entire communities and vast quantities of supplies. The robot helps to preserve an image of what has been lost in the move to the new environment, whether it be the imaginative traditions of literature ("Usher II") or the stable family unit ("The Long Years"). These machines are equally alien to the Midwestern society of Bradbury's characters and the fantasy landscape of Mars. As such, they heighten what Suvin calls our "cognitive estrangement" from both the "real" world and the imagined landscape of Mars. Mars cannot entirely be a fantasy world, since machines can take us to it. Neither can the familiar society of the American Midwest be completely real, since it features these fanciful machines. So we are left feeling slightly alienated from both worlds. This feeling of dual alienation characterized descriptions of the frontier experience in the work of writers well before Bradbury (for example, Willa Cather, a writer he read in the 1940s).

Once Bradbury has established the technological means of exploiting his new frontier, he proceeds to develop the story of colonization along lines that are familiar to any American reader. The parallels between the conquest of Mars and the conquest of the American Indians have been noted by several commentators, including Sam Lundwall, who regards *The Martian Chronicles* as "a telling example of the American agony of the Indian massacres," while attacking the rest of the book as naive and "crazy." Bradbury himself once claimed in an interview that, in the *Chronicles*, "I pointed out the problems of the Indians, and the Western expansionists." The story of the Martians is only part of the overall narrative implied by the Martian stories, however, just as the conquest of the Indians was only part of advancing the American frontier. What may be less immediately apparent in reading the Martian stories is the way in which Bradbury views the impact of the Martian frontier on American democracy and character, and the ways in which this view reflects earlier views of the American frontier experience, such as that of Frederick Jackson Turner. Bradbury would not claim to be a historical theorist; there isn't much evidence that he is even directly familiar with Turner. But much about the Martian stories—for example, the term *chronicle* itself—suggests that the real subject of the book is history. As Willis E. McNelly recently observed, "Bradbury belongs to the great frontier tradition. He is an exemplar of the Turner thesis, and the blunt opposition between a tradition-bound Eastern establishment and Western vitality finds itself mirrored in his writing." Of course, the Turner thesis itself remains something of an unresolved controversy among historians. First presented at the Chicago World's Fair of 1893, when Turner was a 32-year-old historian at the University of Wisconsin, the paper entitled "The Significance of the Frontier in American History" offered a radical departure from the teachings of earlier historians who had sought to explain American history primarily in terms of European influence. Instead, Turner argued, American development could best be explained by the existence of a continually receding frontier area of sparsely settled land, a frontier that had officially ceased to exist with the 1890 census. During the next thirty to forty years this thesis became one of the most famous and controversial pieces of writing in the field of American history. Historians, sociologists, and literary critics either attacked or vigorously defended it. Turner himself returned to the theme again and again, perhaps most notably with his 1903 essay, "Contributions of the West to American Democracy." Whatever the merits of the thesis, its influence became so widespread in the teaching and writing of American history and literature that few today have not been affected by it. It is worth noting that the Turner thesis was probably at the height of its influence during Ray Bradbury's formative years.

Just to what extent it can be said that Bradbury is an exemplar of the Turner thesis or of the frontier imagination which the thesis represents, is the focus of the rest of this chapter. Turner, like Bradbury, believed the wilderness could transform the colonists. He regarded the frontier as a kind of safety valve for American development: "Whenever social conditions tended to press upon labor or political restraints to impede the freedom of the mass, there was this gate of escape to the free conditions of the frontier. These free lands promoted individualism, economic equality, freedom to rise, democracy." Such qualities, in turn, provided a check on the growing institutionalization and industrialization of life in the urbanized East. But with the closing of the frontier, Turner saw an era of American life come to an end. (A later historian, Walter Prescott Webb, viewed the closing of the frontier on an even grander scale, characterizing it as the end of a "Great Frontier" that had governed European and American expansion for over 400 years.) If, as Turner claimed, the major aspects of American democracy had developed largely because of the continual existence of the area of free land, then there was a danger that these values might be lost as the rise of increasingly complex industrial and governmental bureaucracies continued without this safety valve. Turner saw the rise of captains of industry and politics as replacing the old Western heroes. He even made an unconvincing attempt to portray Carnegie, Field, and Rockefeller as pioneers of a sort, but in the end felt that it was "still to be determined whether these men constitute a menace to democratic institutions, or [are] the most efficient factor for adjusting democratic control to the new conditions."

Bradbury apparently regarded such men (or their descendants) as a menace. The increasingly antidemocratic society of Earth (portrayed in greater detail in *Fahrenheit 451*, elements of which can also be seen in the Martian stories) is what drives many of the colonists to Mars. Near the end of "The Million-Year Picnic," the father burns the stock market graphs, government pamphlets, and military documents that had come to symbolize life on Earth. Like Turner, Bradbury felt that the society he most valued was in danger from encroaching governmental restrictions. Bradbury singles out the censorship of comic books: "They begin by controlling books of cartoons and then detective books and, of course, films, one way or another, one group or another, political bias, religious prejudice, union pressures; there was always a minority afraid of something, and a great majority afraid of the dark, afraid of the future, afraid of the past, afraid of the present, afraid of themselves and shadows of themselves." With the culture of his Midwestern boyhood thus endangered, Bradbury's Mars becomes an escape valve in much the same way as Turner's West.

Here I do not mean to suggest that Bradbury's, or even Turner's, depiction of social forces is defensible in terms of modern historical theory, or that Bradbury's book is, in any way, a deliberate outgrowth or illustration of

Turner's thesis. There are many points at which Bradbury's frontier diverges from that of Turner or goes beyond it; in addition, the hazards of overzealous application of Turner's thesis are already familiar to students of American literature. As Henry Nash Smith and others have pointed out, Turner's frontier was largely a codification of an agrarian myth—the myth of the garden—that had long been in the air of American intellectual life. The notion of the West as safety valve, almost universally accepted during the nineteenth century, is not supported by solid evidence. But Smith also points out that, partly because of the power of the traditions underlying Turner's thesis, "it has been worked into the very fabric of our conception of history," becoming part of the common folklore of Americans' ideas about their past. That Bradbury is rooted in this tradition is revealed most clearly by examining some of the similarities between his ideas and Turner's.

The broad similarities between Bradbury and Turner are apparent to any reader familiar with both men. In *The Martian Chronicles* it is tempting to read the Earth as the industrial East, Mars as the frontier West, the Martians as Indians, and the humans as frontiersmen and women. As a narrative, the *Chronicles* is not consistent enough to support such a broad equation. The Martian stories not included in the *Chronicles*, but which explore the same issues in different ways, further complicate the situation. What is more to the point is the general flow of ideas in Bradbury's Martian stories, particularly the relationship between available frontier lands and the concept of democracy that is significant in both Turner and Bradbury.

In both writers the emergence of a frontier society is portrayed in a series of distinct stages. First, there is the initial exploratory stage in which the inhabitants of the frontier environment are encountered and subdued. In the second stage the environment masters the colonist, transforming him into a kind of native with new values. Third is the successive waves of subsequent settlers who begin to develop towns and commerce. Finally there are those who see in the frontier an opportunity to correct the mistakes of the past and escape the oppression of the urbanized environment they have left behind.

The first stage is characterized by Turner's definition of the frontier as "the meeting point between savagery and civilization." If we remember that for Turner, the word *savagery* encompassed the civilization of the American Indians, we can see that this idea also dominates the first section of *The Martian Chronicles*, those episodes that deal with the confrontation between Earthmen and Martians. Unlike Turner and most writers of frontier fiction, however, Bradbury offers a dual perspective. Martian society is initially portrayed as a kind of caricature of middle-class institutions; like Bradbury's Indian fables, the book begins with the natives' point of view. The first stories, then, are not stories of adventure in unknown realms, much as we might expect in a story of the exploration of Mars, but rather are stories of outside interlopers disturbing the placidity of a stable, conservative society. It is one of the more successful ironies of the book that the first Earthmen are killed not by monsters but by a jealous husband, and that the second expedition dies at the hands of an unreasoning bureaucracy. These are the only clear glimpses we have of Martian civilization, however, for in "The Third Expedition" the Martians emerge as duplicitous monsters planning with elaborate premeditation the destruction of the visitors from Earth. But even in this story it is less the Martians who do in the explorers than the explorers' own past—their persistent willingness to believe in the unlikely reality of their own childhoods being reconstructed on a distant planet. It is this persistence of the past, this trap of the old values of civilization, that initially destroys the unprepared explorer on the alien frontier. Ironically, it may also contribute to the destruction of the Martians themselves, as in the story "The Martian" or the non-*Chronicle* story "The Messiah" (1971), both of which depict telepathic Martians unwittingly transforming themselves into images drawn from the memories of the humans around them.

Bradbury makes little attempt in these early stories to point up the parallels between the situation of the Martians and that of the American Indians. In "—And the Moon Be Still as Bright," however, he introduces a character who is at least part Indian. Cheroke, one of the members of the Fourth Expedition, is asked how he would feel if he "were a Martian and people came to your land and started tearing it up." He replies: "I know exactly how I'd feel . . . I've got some Cherokee blood in me. My grandfather told me lots of things about Oklahoma Territory. If there's a Martian around, I'm all for him."

Unknown to Cheroke, there *is* a Martian around. Spender, a member of the crew, is so taken with the dead Martian civilization (*dead* because of the chicken pox brought by earlier Earthmen) that he comes to regard himself as "the last Martian," the appointed protector of Martian lands from invading Earthmen. The transformation of Spender introduces the second major stage of frontier experience, one that has been developed by Bradbury in many ways in stories both in and out of the *Chronicles.* This is the stage in which the environment transforms the settler into a kind of native:

> The wilderness masters the colonist. It finds him a European in
> dress, industries, tools, modes of travel, and thought. It takes him
> from the railroad car and puts him in the birch canoe. It strips off
> the garments of civilization and arrays him in the hunting shirt and

the moccasin. It puts him in the log cabin of the Cherokee and Iroquois and runs an Indian palisade around him. . . . In short, at the frontier the environment is at first too strong for the man.

Spender is the first exemplar of this kind of transformation to appear in the Martian stories. Significantly, Cheroke is the one he invites to join him in his crusade to protect the Martian wilderness. When Cheroke refuses to join Spender's scheme to murder all of the settlers, he is killed. Captain Wilder, however, feels sympathy for Spender's position; it is to the captain that Spender defends his actions by comparing Mars to the Indian civilizations of Mexico before the invasion of Cortez: "A whole civilization destroyed by greedy, righteous bigots. History will never forgive Cortez." It is partly out of sympathy for Spender's viewpoint that the captain knocks the teeth out of a callous crew member who uses the fragile Martian towers for target practice. But Wilder is not a settler; he is an explorer. For most of the time frame covered by the *Chronicles*, he is off exploring other parts of the solar system. "I've been out to Jupiter and Saturn and Neptune for twenty years," he tells former crew member Hathaway in "The Long Years." Thus, like such early frontiersmen as Daniel Boone, Captain Wilder is capable of maintaining a balanced view of frontier development because he isn't really a part of it; he is continually moving beyond into still more distant frontiers.

Spender lacks this distance, though. "When I got up here I felt I was not only free of their so-called culture, I felt I was free of their ethics and their customs. I'm out of their frame of reference, I thought. All I have to do is kill you all off and live my own life." The overpowering beauty of the fantasy environment of Mars, and the freedom this environment represents, have indeed "mastered the colonist." The notion of Mars transforming its settlers, either literally or figuratively, becomes a major theme in subsequent Martian stories and the dominant theme in at least two of them.

"The Million-Year Picnic" and "Dark They Were, and Golden Eyed" were published in magazine form before the *Chronicles* were collected, "Picnic" in 1946 and "Dark They Were" in 1949. Both stories further develop the theme of settlers being transformed by the Martian environment; but only "Picnic" was included in the *Chronicles*. "The Naming of Names," the magazine title of "Dark They Were," survives only as the title of an interim passage in the *Chronicles*; the story itself did not appear in book form until A *Medicine for Melancholy* in 1959. Although the story takes place on the same Mars as the *Chronicles*, it was excluded apparently because of its central fantastic device—some element in the Martian soil or atmosphere that physically transforms Earthmen into Martians—appears in no other Martian story and would have destroyed the illusion of a unified narrative that Bradbury was trying to achieve. (In another non-*Chronicles* Mars story also published in 1949, "The One Who Waits," Earthmen are literally possessed by the intelligence of an ancient Martian who lives in a well.)

"The Million-Year Picnic" is an appropriate, if predictable, ending for *The Martian Chronicles*, one not very subtle in preparing the reader for the final revelation that the "Martians" Dad has been promising to show the family are the reflection of the family itself in the water of a canal. But the ending is more than a narrative trick; throughout the story we are given hints that the family is adapting to its new environment—so thoroughly, in fact, that the eventual destruction of Earth seems to have less emotional impact on the children than the death of a pet canary might. The first accommodation to the new environment occurs in the story's opening scene: the family has left its "family rocket," which seems to have been a common recreational vehicle on Earth ("Family rockets are made for travel to the Moon, not Mars"), for a motorboat, still a mechanical product of Earth technology but one that is better suited for travel on the canals of Mars. Father tells the children they are going fishing. Perhaps this is merely a ruse to get them away from the rocket so he can blow it up; nonetheless, it is the kind of activity that takes on a different meaning in a frontier environment by becoming a means of sustenance rather than sport. They come upon a dead Martian city. Dad "looked as if he was pleased that it was dead." Is Dad pleased because he is trying to escape the riotous urban life represented by cities on Earth, or because he sees it as an example of the abundant resources available to settlers in this new land, or because it represents the failure of the colonists before them to found large communities on Mars? Whatever the reason, the father's motivation is akin to that of one of Turner's pioneers. His supplies are also the supplies of a pioneer—extensive provisions and a gun. The radio, the only means of contact with the dying Earth, soon becomes useless.

What we see in these images of recreational vehicles, picnics, fishing trips, radios, and the like is the gradual transformation of the icons of American leisure culture into patterns of survival in the new land. As the story progresses, the "picnic" becomes less a family outing than a metaphor for the eventual rebirth of a new civilization. The finite event of a vacation becomes infinite; play becomes life, the basis of which is focused on the new Martian environment rather than memories of Earth. Every member of the family begins to think in these new terms, and Bradbury's metaphors take on a Martian focus. Dad's face looks like "one of those fallen Martian cities," and his breathing sounds like the lapping of waters against the stone walls of the Martian canals. Earlier his eyes had reminded one of the boys of "agate marbles you play with after school in summer back on Earth." Dad has become more "Martian" in the eyes of his children, who do not yet realize what is going on.

In choosing a city for settlement, the family rejects one that appears to be an Earth settlement. In sharp contrast to the enthusiastic embracing of the past by the crew members in the earlier story, "The Third Expedition," the rejection of the past in "The Million-Year Picnic" is yet another sign of the family's transformation. When they finally choose a city—a Martian city—the radio, their last contact with Earth, goes dead. "No more Minneapolis, no more rockets, no more Earth," explains Dad in a synecdoche that subsumes the very existence of the planet into images of cities and rockets, suggesting that "Earth" has become less a planet in his mind than a way of life to be rejected. He completes the separation with a ceremonial burning of Earth documents: "I'm burning a way of life, just like that way of life is being burned clean of Earth right now," going on to berate politics, science, technology—the evils of the East that Turner's pioneers found themselves rejecting. "Even if there hadn't been a war," Dad says, "we would have come to Mars, I think, to live and form our own standard of living." The orientation toward a new world that we have sensed developing throughout the story is finally shown to be an orientation that took root on Earth—a desire to escape urbanization and technology, to settle on a frontier that no longer existed on Earth. Thus it is hardly a surprise when the Martians are finally revealed to us. What is revealed is merely the first step of a family's self-consciousness as pioneer settlers.

If "Dark They Were, and Golden-Eyed" had been included in the *Chronicles*, "The Million-Year Picnic" would have been rendered impossible by the assumptions of the former story. But the latter also deals with the theme of the transforming frontier, of Earthmen becoming Martians. In "Dark They Were," the transformation is literal; the overpowering influence of the environment is the central feature. Like "Picnic," "Dark They Were" begins with a family leaving its rocket to settle on Mars; but this time the environment has an immediate and ominous effect. The father feels "the tissues of his body draw tight as if he were standing at the center of a vacuum." His wife seems "almost to whirl away in smoke," and the children, as "small seeds, might at any instant be sown to all the Martian climes." "The wind blew as if to flake away their identities. At any moment the Martian air might draw his [the father's] soul from him, as marrow comes from a white bone. He felt submerged in a chemical that could dissolve his intellect and burn away his past." The father later says he feels "like a salt crystal in a mountain stream, being washed away." The family establishes itself in a cottage on Mars, but the fear of being transformed by the alien environment remains. Trying to be cheerful, the father describes their experience as "colonial days all over again" and looks forward to the coming colonization of Mars and the development of "Big cities, everything!" Earth values are in no way rejected by these settlers, unlike those in "The Million-Year Picnic"; and the ancient Martian names of natural formations are replaced by names of American political and industrial leaders—"Hormel Valleys, Roosevelt Seas, Ford Hills, Vanderbilt Plateaus, Rockefeller Rivers." Although the father begins to feel that the American settlers had shown greater wisdom in using Indian names, he is not yet ready to reject this culture. In an effort to transform the Martian environment into something familiar, he plants flowers and vegetables from Earth.

None of this works, of course. It is reminiscent of Nathaniel Hawthorne's governor whose attempts to grow a traditional European garden in the new world are thwarted by wild pumpkin vines. The plants take on Martian characteristics, and when—as in "The Million-Year Picnic"—an atomic war on Earth strands the settlers, these transformations include the settlers, too. Eventually the family abandons its earthly goods and moves into an abandoned Martian city where they speak the extinct Martian language, finally turning physically into a family of Martians with no more interest in Earth and its affairs. The environment has totally mastered the colonists. When, after the atomic war, a spaceship arrives from Earth, it finds only a Roanoke-like abandoned colony of Earth buildings.

Interestingly, Bradbury wrote "Dark They Were" three years *after* "The Million-Year Picnic," after the basic structure of the *Chronicles* had begun to take shape from the several stories that were to be included in it. In many ways the story is a reply to and rethinking of "The Million-Year Picnic." It is also one of Bradbury's strongest illustrations of his ideas about environmental determinism. If "The Million-Year Picnic" agrees with Turner's argument that the only way to survive in a frontier environment initially is to adapt to it, "Dark They Were, and Golden-Eyed" goes far beyond either of these in suggesting that the environment completely molds the settler in its own image. The family in "The Million-Year Picnic" chooses the Martian way of life; the family in "Dark They Were, and Golden-Eyed" has no such choice.

In a sense, Bradbury's Martian frontier never moves beyond the stage of environmental domination (the theme is strongly stated in the last story of the book). But in other stories Bradbury does describe later stages of settlement; it is a description that is remarkably similar to Turner's account of the farming frontier of the West. According to Turner, "the farmer's advance came in a distinct series of waves"; while Bradbury writes "Mars was a distant shore, and the men spread upon it in waves" (in the *Chronicles*). Turner describes the frontier as, successively, the realm of the hunter, followed by the trader, the rancher, the farmer, and finally the manufacturer. He alludes to a still earlier writer on the Western frontier, John Mason Peck, whose 1837 *New Guide to the West* lists the stages of frontier growth as moving from the pioneer to the settler to the businessman. Bradbury describes the first men as "coyote and cattle men" from the Midwest, followed by urban Easterners from "cabbage tenements and subways."

> The second men should have traveled from other countries with other accents and other ideas. But the rockets were American and the men were American and its stayed that way, while Europe and Asia and South America and Australia and the islands watched the Roman candles leave them behind. The rest of the world was buried in war or the thoughts of war.

The rather weak rationale that other countries were too involved in war to undertake space exploration hardly seems consistent with the American cold-war mentality we see criticized in other parts of the book (such as "Usher II" and "The Million-Year Picnic"). A simpler explanation is that Bradbury, like Turner, conceived of the frontier as a uniquely American experience, an extension of a movement that had characterized the nation since its beginning.

In a Martian story written after the *Chronicles* was published, Bradbury develops his notion of later frontier development by exploring the reactions of two women preparing to join their husbands on Mars. "The Wilderness" (1952; collected in *The Golden Apples of the Sun*) opens in Independence, Missouri (the starting point for 1849 Western colonists) with "a sound like a steamboat down the river" which turns out to be a rocket. As this setting and image suggest, virtually the entire story is built around the parallels between the Martian settlement and the earlier westward movement. An old Wyoming song is modified to fit the Martian adventure, and the trip to Mars is contrasted with an earlier generation's trip "from Fort Laramie to Hangtown." The story is slight in terms of narrative; but its ending, in which one of the women meditates on her journey to Mars the next morning, gives us Bradbury's clearest deliberate parallel between the two frontiers, which may also suggest why the parallel is so strong:

> Is this how it was over a century ago, she wondered, when the women, the night before, lay ready for sleep, or not ready, in the small towns of the East, and heard the sound of horses in the night and the creak of the Conestoga wagons ready to go,

and the brooding of oxen under the trees, and the cry of children already lonely before their time? All the sounds of arrivals and departures into the deep forests and fields, the blacksmiths working in their own red hells through midnight? And the smell of bacons and hams ready for the journeying, and the heavy feel of the wagons like ships foundering with goods, with water in the wooden kegs to tilt across the prairies, and the chickens hysterical in their slung-beneath-the-wagon crates, and the dogs running out to the wilderness ahead and, fearful, running back with a look of empty space in their eyes? Is this, then, how it was so long ago? On the rim of the precipice, on the edge of the cliff of stars. In their time the smell of buffalo, and in our time the smell of the Rocket. Is this, then, how it was?

Note that, of all the richly detailed, sensuous imagery in this passage, the only image that is in any way associated with space travel is "the smell of the Rocket." Janice (the character whose meditation this is) seems far more aware of the sensuous details of a romantic past than of her own environment. In general, Bradbury's work relies more on such images than on attempts to create a sense of future time through imagery and detail. But for Janice—and perhaps for Bradbury, as well—it is only by dwelling on these images that one can arrive at some sort of resolution of the conflicts generated by the idea of traveling to another world. The unknown, uncertain future is validated by the parallels with a familiar past: "this was as it had always been and would forever continue to be." Unlike the earlier pioneer settlers, for whom the past is destructive, or the family in "The Million-Year Picnic" who finally achieve liberation from the past, this intermediate group of settlers can conceptualize the alien experience of a new world only by drawing on memories of pleasant past experiences. Hence we have spaceships seen as tin cans or Roman candles, space as an ocean, Martian villages as small Midwestern towns, and Martians themselves as figures from one's life on Earth. Although Turner does not focus on the role of the past in frontier experience, for Bradbury it is a necessary way of dealing with the new environment.

The stage of frontier experience common to Turner and Bradbury is that where the frontier begins to exert a democratizing influence on the settlers. In Turner, this influence is felt throughout the East, as well as in the West, as a general force moving America toward a more open and democratic society. But in Bradbury, there is no real commerce between Earth and Mars, and therefore no cultural "feedback" of this sort (if one were to examine this critically, he might conclude that the economics of *The Martian*

Chronicles is as fatuous as its science). Bradbury shares with Turner some shaky assumptions about how the frontier works by its very presence against oppression. For example, both men naively assume that the frontier helps alleviate racial problems—Bradbury with his story "Way in the Middle of the Air" and Turner with his statement that "the free pioneer democracy struck down the slaveholding aristocracy on its march to the West." Bradbury's blacks are actually part of a larger group of colonists who view Mars as a place to escape the oppression and reassert democratic principles (though the blacks themselves are tempted to indulge in this kind of oppression in "The Other Foot," a story in *The Illustrated Man* that serves as a sequel to "Way in the Middle of the Air"). Other representatives of this group of stories include figures as diverse as Stendahl in "Usher II," the father in "The Million-Year Picnic," and Parkhill in "The Off-Season" (not a sympathetic character but nonetheless a small-time capitalist who, like many who move to the frontier, sees such a move as his greatest opportunity for free enterprise).

Turner writes:

> But the most important effect of the frontier has been in the promotion of democracy here and in Europe. As has been indicated, the frontier is productive of individualism. Complex society is precipitated by the wilderness into a kind of primitive organization based on the family. The tendency is anti-social. It produces antipathy to control, and particularly to any direct control. The tax-gatherer is viewed as a representative of oppression.

This antisocial, family-oriented tendency of frontier settlement is perhaps most clearly represented in "The Million-Year Picnic," though the tendency appears in "Usher II" as well. Stendahl, an independently wealthy eccentric who "came to Mars to get away from . . . Clean-Minded people"—the powerful censors and enforcers of "moral climates" who are descendants of the comic-book censors of the fifties—is actually a fugitive from the society of *Fahrenheit 451* and a precursor of Montag in that novel. Stendahl, who on earth had seen his cache of books incinerated by Moral Climate investigators, views Mars as an opportunity to reassert his freedom of speech and gain revenge while doing it. With the assistance of Pikes, a former actor in horror movies, he reconstructs the House of Usher according to Poe's description and uses it to trap members of the Society for the Prevention of Fantasy— "the Spoil-Funs, the people with mercurochrome for blood and iodine-colored eyes." One by one, they are killed off in a manner described in Poe's stories, and are then replaced by robots. Eventually, Stendahl escapes in his helicopter and heads (perhaps significantly) west.

In this story—as in another Martian story not included in the *Chronicles* ("The Exiles," in which the spirits of imaginative writers survive on Mars until the last copies of their books are burned)—Bradbury seems to go beyond Turner in arguing for the significance of the frontier in a democracy. Whereas Turner confined his account of the frontier influence to certain social and political traits that pushed America toward democracy, Bradbury seems to suggest that democratic thought can be measured simply by freedom of imagination; that, more than anything else, the frontier is a haven for imaginative thought. Only on Mars can imagination be liberated and restored to the daily conduct of life. Bradbury seems to be saying that, as society becomes more and more complex, the role of fantasy is increasingly left out; but as society is simplified by the limited resources of a new environment, the fantasy returns. Thus Stendahl's master stroke is not merely the murder of the censors but the fact that this murder is carried out by robots—mechanical devices which are part of the culture that repressed fantasy in the first place.

This brings us back to Bradbury's attitude toward machines. We have seen how machines such as the rocket contribute to the colonization of Mars, but not how technology has oppressed and degraded life on Earth, thus creating a society against which Bradbury can develop his democratizing frontier. "And There Will Come Soft Rains" gives us some clues. The shadow images of the dead family on the outer wall of the mechanical house, in contrast to the ingeniously programmed robots that continue to perform their daily chores within, strongly suggest the directions technology has taken: its deliberate degradation of life by the proliferation of "cute" labor-saving gadgets, and the immense, unchecked power represented by the bomb. Ultimately, both kinds of development are stagnant; both represent failures of the earthbound imagination. Just as the bomb locks international relations into a cold war, so do the gadgets lock family life into a mechanical parody of the suburban life style. Each in its own way oppresses the imagination and the freedom which that imagination represents, a freedom that can be reborn only on the frontier.

Strength of imagination, then, becomes the key to survival on Bradbury's frontier—the ability to achieve the new perspective demanded by the new environment. Few of Bradbury's characters are capable of this; at the end of the *Chronicles*, nearly all the settlers return to the dying Earth, unwilling or unable to cut the umbilical cord to the past. As the proprietor in "The Luggage Store" says:

> "I know, we came up here to get away from things—politics, the
> atom bomb, war, pressure groups, prejudice, laws—I know. But

it's still home there. You wait and see. When the first bomb drops
on America the people up here'll start thinking. They haven't
been here long enough. A couple of years is all. If they'd been
here forty years, it'd be different, but they got relatives down
there, and their home towns."

In other words, the frontier hasn't yet "taken"; most settlers are not yet
ready to think of themselves as Martians. When the pleas to return home
arrive in appropriately frontier fashion—Morse code—they abandon the
new world. When asked to explain his rationale for having the settlers
return in the face of atomic war, Bradbury replied: "we had just come out
of World War II, where a hell of a lot of foreigners went home to be killed.
They could have stayed in the United States." A similar analogy might be
made to the number of western settlers who returned to fight in the American Civil War, which interrupted the settlement of the West in much the
same way that atomic war interrupts the settlement of Mars. In any event,
the liberating, democratizing influences of Bradbury's frontier is never
given a chance to develop its full potential. We are left with a few isolated
settlements, only one of which—the family in "The Million-Year Picnic"—
realizes the Martian promise of freedom.

In "The Highway," a story published the same year as *The Martian
Chronicles*, Bradbury describes a Mexican peasant who is puzzled when he
finds the highway beside his hut crowded with cars filled with Americans
frantically heading north. One of the Americans stops for water, and the
peasant asks the reason for the sudden migration homeward. "It's come,"
responds the American, "the atom war, the end of the world!" As in *The
Martian Chronicles*, the Americans choose to go home to almost certain death
rather than stay in Mexico. Unimpressed by the talk of nuclear war, the
peasant returns to his plow, muttering: "What do they mean, 'the world?'"
What indeed? After all, "the world" is nothing more than what an individual's perspective makes it—circumscribed by a plot of land for a Mexican
peasant, defined as a way of life by an American in an alien land. In both
"The Exiles" and *The Martian Chronicles* the "end of the world" is actually
the destruction of America, of the culture that gave birth to the myth of the
frontier. With the end of this culture, Mars ceases to exist as a frontier, as the
leading edge of a growing civilization. If, as Henry Nash Smith suggests,
Turner's myth of the frontier—which, as we have seen, is shared by Bradbury—did have its foundations in the Edenic myth of the new world, then
the conclusion of *The Martian Chronicles* brings the myth full circle. In "The
Million-Year Picnic," what was once the frontier land of Mars literally
becomes the new Eden, giving birth to a new human civilization out of the

ashes of the old. Two civilizations have died to make this new birth possible, and we are left with the slight hope that the new one will synthesize what was best about the Martian and Earth societies. The frontier sensibility that has governed most of the book is replaced by a utopian sensibility. We can only speculate as to the society Bradbury hoped to evolve from his five lonely Martians, staring at themselves in the rippling water of a Martian canal.

KEVIN HOSKINSON

Ray Bradbury's Cold War Novels

In a discussion about the thematic content of *The Martian Chronicles* with interviewer David Mogen in 1980, Ray Bradbury stated, "*The Martian Chronicles* and *Fahrenheit 451* come from the same period in my life, when I was warning people. I was *preventing* futures." In this pairing of the two books, Bradbury suggests a deep kinship between the pieces and indicates the probability that they are more than just successive novels in his overall body of work. Though the two fictions are usually read as separate entities, if read as complementary works, they provide a more comprehensive view of a larger whole. As consecutive arrivals in Bradbury's postwar publications, and in their mutual attraction to similar major themes of the cold war era, *The Martian Chronicles* and *Fahrenheit 451* distinguish themselves as Bradbury's "cold war novels."

The two works are on the surface entirely different kinds of fiction. *The Martian Chronicles* is a collection of twenty-six chapters (most originally published as short stories), written between 1944 and 1950 and linked primarily by their setting on the planet Mars between the years 1999 and 2026. Since many of the stories were separately conceived, most of the characters in the finished book are contained within their individual tales and do not cross over into other chapters. And though Mars itself is in many ways the centerpiece of the book, and its treatment by the humans is "chronicled"

From *Extrapolation* 36, no. 4. © 1995 by The Kent State University Press. (Originally published as "*The Martian Chronicles* and *Fahrenheit 451:* Ray Bradbury's Cold War Novels.")

over a twenty-seven-year period, there is no "protagonist" in the pure sense of the term, nor is there a "plot" common to the separate sections. In contrast, *Fahrenheit 451* is structured as a novel, divided into three chapters; it is set on Earth; it is the story of one central protagonist, Guy Montag; and the plot of the novel—Montag's liberation from Captain Beatty and his acceptance of a new purpose in a new civilization—is carefully mapped out.

These surface differences of structure, character, and setting notwithstanding, *The Martian Chronicles* and *Fahrenheit 451* share a distinction as "cold war fiction" because in them, much more deliberately than in earlier or later publications, Bradbury deals with subjects and issues that were shaped by the political climate of the United States in the decade immediately following World War II. A number of significant events during these years transformed the character of America from a supremely confident, Nazi-demolishing world leader to a country with deep insecurities, one suddenly suspicious and vigilant of Communist activity within its citizenry. First, Joseph Stalin's immediate and unchecked occupation of Eastern European countries at the close of World War II left many Americans wondering if the United States and the Roosevelt administration hadn't foolishly misjudged Soviet intentions at the Yalta Conference in 1945. Second, the Soviet Union's subsequent acquisition of atomic weapons technology by 1949 would reinforce this position; it would also end the U.S. monopoly on thermonuclear weapons and raise questions about Communist agents in high-level government positions. Third, Senator Joseph McCarthy's public accusations of Communist activity in the State Department in 1950 (together with the inflammatory tactics of J. Edgar Hoover, the FBI, and a host of other right-wing government agencies) planted seeds of paranoia and subversion in the American culture that would blossom into fear and irrationality throughout the 1950s. As David Halberstam points out, "It was a mean time. The nation was ready for witch-hunts." Through his examination of government oppression of the individual, the hazards of an atomic age, recivilization of society, and the divided nature of the "Cold War Man," Ray Bradbury uses *The Martian Chronicles* and *Fahrenheit 451* to expose the "meanness" of the cold war years.

During the Truman years of the early cold war, when the administration attempted to reverse the image of the Democratic party as being "soft" on communism, the U.S. government attempted to silence individuals who were thought to be "potentially disloyal" through various offices such as the Justice Department and the Loyalty Review Board. ⟨Historian Alan Theoharis notes that⟩ Truman himself released a press statement in July 1950 that granted authority over national security matters to the FBI. The statement expressed grave concern over "the Godless Communist Cause" and further warned that "it is important to learn to know the enemies of the American way of life." For Bradbury, such government-supported conformism amounted to censorship and ultimately led to the fostering of what William F. Touponce labels "mass culture" and what Kingsley Amis calls "conformist hell." We see Bradbury's strong distrust of "majority-held" views and official doctrine positions in several places in *The Martian Chronicles*; these areas of distrust, moreover, recur in *Fahrenheit 451*.

In the seventh chapter of *Chronicles*, "—And the Moon Be Still as Bright" (originally published in 1948), the fierceness of the individual and the official will of the majority clash violently in the persons of Jeff Spender and Captain Wilder. Spender is a crewman on the Fourth Expedition to Mars who feels a sense of moral outrage at the behavior of his fellow crewmen upon landing. While Biggs, Parkhill, and others break out the liquor and throw a party upon their successful mission, Spender is revolted at their dancing and their harmonica playing on the Martian landscape and at Biggs's throwing of wine bottles into canals and vomiting on the tiled city floors. Spender marvels at Martian literature and ancient art forms, and he views the others' actions as sacrilegious, lamenting that "We Earth Men have a talent for ruining big, beautiful things." Like Spender, Captain Wilder also perceives the beauty of the cities; but as the officer of the crew, he does not allow his sympathies with Spender to override his need as commander in chief to preserve authoritative control of the mission. He doles out a perfunctory fifty-dollar fine to Spender for punching Biggs and orders Spender to "go back [to the party] and play happy"; later, following Spender's desertion and mutinous killing of several crewmen, Wilder acknowledges that he has "too much earth blood" to accept Spender's invitation to stay on Mars without the others. Wilder is convinced by this time that he must stop Spender, but he is tormented by an uncertainty over whether he is stopping him because he believes Spender is wrong or whether he simply lacks Spender's individual conviction to lash out against the will of the majority: "I hate this feeling of thinking I'm doing right when I'm not really certain I am. Who are we, anyway? The majority? Is that the answer? . . . What is this majority and who are in it? And what do they think and how did they get that way and will they ever change and how the devil did I get caught in this rotten majority? I don't feel comfortable." In order to preclude the disintegration of the mission, Wilder shoots Spender before Spender can kill anyone else. But the issue of individuality vs. conformity that has been raised by Spender's mutiny has not been resolved for the captain. The next day, Wilder knocks out Parkhill's teeth after Parkhill has shot out the windows of some of the buildings in a dead city. Wilder here releases his inner rage at his own ambivalent compliance with a "government finger point[ing] from four-color posters" described in the book's next chapter, "The Settlers." On the one hand, he has eliminated the disruptive presence of an outlaw; on the other hand, in so doing he has taken the Official Position and removed from the expedition the value of "the most renegade of Bradbury's frontiersmen" (Mogen) as well as the one other individual who valued art and creative expression.

Bradbury picks up this theme of distrust for the officially endorsed view again in "Usher II," the seventeenth chapter of *Chronicles* (originally published in 1950 prior to the publication of the full book). In this chapter William Stendahl designs a replica of Edgar Allan Poe's House of Usher on Mars. His intent is twofold: to pay tribute to Poe and "to teach [the Clean-Minded people] a fine lesson for what [they] did to Mr. Poe on Earth," which was to burn his works (along with the works of others who wrote "tales of the future") in the Great Fire of 1975. Here again Bradbury rejects the will of the majority through Stendahl's speech to Bigelow, the architect of Usher II. Stendahl sermonizes to Bigelow that the Great Fire came about because "there was always a minority afraid of something, and a great majority afraid of the dark, afraid of the future, afraid of the past, afraid of the present, afraid of themselves and shadows of themselves." Another neurosis Bradbury places in Stendahl's litany of fears has roots in the "red scare" policies enacted through McCarthyist tactics in 1950s America: "Afraid of the word 'politics' (which eventually became a synonym for Communism among the more reactionary elements, so I hear, and it was worth your life to use the word!) . . ." Later, at the party Stendahl throws for his invited guests, the Moral Climates people, Stendahl kills all the "majority guests" with different approaches to murders seen in Poe's stories. At the end of the chapter, Stendahl mortars up Moral Climates Investigator Garrett into a brick wall because Garrett "took other people's advice that [Poe's books] needed burning." In contrast with "—And the Moon Be Still as Bright," where the individual is martyred by the majority, the individual in "Usher II" enjoys a sinister triumph over the majority.

In *Fahrenheit 451* Bradbury resumes his attack on government-based censorship encountered earlier in "Usher II." Set on Earth rather than on Mars, this novel follows the metamorphosis of Guy Montag, a fireman (a starter of fires in this future dystopian society) who comes to question and break free of the government that employs him to burn books. The novel opens with Montag having just returned to the firehouse after igniting another residence, "grinn[ing] the fierce grin of all men singed and driven back by flame." He is clearly of the majority at this point, loyal to his job and proud of wearing the salamander and the phoenix disc, the official insignia of the Firemen of America. But seventeen-year-old Clarisse McClellan, who is dangerous in Beatty's eyes because "she [doesn't] want to know *how* a thing [is] done, but *why*," points out some disturbing facts that Montag cannot escape: he answers her questions quickly without thinking; he can't remember if he knew there was dew on early-morning grass or not; he can't answer the question of whether he is happy or not. A growing unrest with his own lack of individual sensibilities creeps into Montag at Clarisse's challenges. As Donald Watt observes, Clarisse is "catalytic" and "dominant in Montag's growth to awareness"; her role for Montag parallels the role of Spender for Captain Wilder, planting the seed of doubt that enacts a process of critical self-examination. These doubts about the government he is serving accumulate through the latest suicide attempt by Montag's wife, Mildred (and her casual acceptance of this attempt after she is resuscitated); through his witnessing of a book-hoarding woman who chose to ignite her own home rather than flee in the face of the firemen's flamethrowers; through the government's systematic elimination of Clarisse; through his own growing need to read and understand books.

Montag ultimately realizes that he cannot return to the firehouse. At this point he rejects both the realm of the majority and his association with Chief Beatty, who professes to "stand against the small tide of those who want to make everyone unhappy with conflicting theory and thought." Montag's liberation from the Firemen of America is augmented when he locates Faber (a former English professor and current member of the book-preserving underground), who offers Montag moral counsel and employs him as an infiltrator at the firehouse. Mildred, in the meantime, breaks her silence and sounds a fire alarm at the Montag residence. In a dramatic confrontation of Individual vs. State, Montag refuses Beatty's orders to burn his own house and instead turns the flamethrower on Beatty. This revolt severs Montag from the majority permanently; he then joins the underground movement to preserve books for the future as global war descends on the city.

Another theme of the cold war years Bradbury takes up in both novels is the precariousness of human existence in an atomic age. The eventual "success" of the Manhattan Project in 1945, which resulted in the development of the atomic bomb, came about only after several years' worth of blind groping toward the right physics equations by some of the brightest physicists in the world. The scientists were literally guessing about how to detonate the bomb, how big to make the bomb, and, most significantly, how strong the bomb would be. The project itself, in the words of Lansing Lamont, was "a bit like trying to manufacture a new automobile with no opportunity to test the engine beforehand." After studying various reports on a wide range of explosions in known history, the Los Alamos physicists determined that the atom bomb's force would fall somewhere in between the volcanic eruption of Krakatau in 1883 (which killed 36,000 people and was heard 3,000 miles away) and the 1917 explosion of the munitions ship *Mont Blanc* in Halifax Harbor, Nova Scotia (killing 1,100)—"hopefully a lot closer to Halifax," Lamont notes, "but just where [the scientists] couldn't be sure." The subsequent explosions at Hiroshima and Nagasaki made Americans more "sure" of the bomb's potential but not sure at all about whether the knowledge of its potential was worth the price of having created it in the first place. As a line of military defense against the spread of nazism, the bomb became a prime example of how science unleashed can, according to Gary Wolfe, produce "the alienation of humanity from the very technological environments it has constructed in order to resolve its alienation from the universe."

It is difficult to comprehend the depth to which the atom bomb terrified the world, and America specifically, in the early cold war era. Richard Rhodes, author of *The Making of the Atomic Bomb*, writes that "A nuclear weapon is in fact a total-death machine, compact and efficient" and quotes a Japanese study that concludes that the explosions at Hiroshima and Nagasaki were "the opening chapter to the annihilation of mankind." More than any single technological development, the atomic bomb made people think seriously about the end of the world. As a passport to Wolfe's icon of the wasteland, the bomb "teaches us that the unknown always remains, ready to reassert itself, to send us back to the beginning."

Bradbury first captures the general sense of anxiety felt in a new atomic age in the fifth chapter of *The Martian Chronicles*, "The Taxpayer." This short chapter identifies fear of nuclear war as an impetus for leaving Earth; the chapter also establishes itself as one of several in *Chronicles* that serve as precursors to *Fahrenheit 451* and centralize many of the early cold war themes Bradbury resumes in the second book: "There was going to be a big atomic war on Earth in about two years, and he didn't want to be here when it happened. He and thousands of others like him, if they had any sense, would go to Mars. See if they wouldn't! To get away from wars and censorship and statism and conscription and government control of this and that, of art and science!"

Once the fear-of-nuclear-holocaust theme is introduced in the book, Bradbury structures the story-chapters so that references to the bomb and to atomic war in *Chronicles* are periodically repeated, thus sustaining anxiety throughout the novel. One of Jeff Spender's fears in "—And the Moon Be Still as Bright," for example, is that war on Earth will lead to "atomic research and atom bomb depots on Mars"; he is willing to kill off the members of the Fourth Expedition in order to keep Earth from "flopping their filthy atom bombs up here, fighting for bases to have wars." "The Luggage Store," a later bridge chapter that echoes the points made in "The Taxpayer," picks up the theme of atomic war on Earth in the year 2005. In discussing whether or not members of the Earth society transplanted on Mars will return to Earth when the war begins, Father Peregrine explains to the proprietor of the luggage store man's inability to comprehend atomic war from millions of miles away: "[Earth is] so far away it's unbelievable. It's not here. You can't touch it. You can't even see it. All you see is a green light. Two billion people living on that light? Unbelievable! War? We don't hear the explosions." The expanse of the physical distance between Earth and Mars in his dialogue mirrors the uneasy diplomatic distance the United States and the Soviet Union managed to somehow sustain throughout the cold war years, which kept atomic war in the abstract then as well.

In November 2005, however, the Mars inhabitants receive a light-radio message in "The Watchers": "AUSTRALIAN CONTINENT ATOMIZED IN PREMA-TURE EXPLOSION OF ATOMIC STOCKPILE. LOS ANGELES, LONDON BOMBED. WAR." The resulting picture of Mars—and Earth—for the remaining forty-two pages of the novel is desolate and, for the most part, apocalyptic. Viewers on Mars could point a telescope at Earth and see New York explode, or London "covered with a new kind of fog." Bradbury also employs humor in driving home the gravity of nuclear catastrophe. In one of the novel's more ironic and darkly humorous chapters, "The Silent Towns," Walter Gripp believes himself the only man left on Mars following the wartime emigration back to Earth by most of the planet's inhabitants. Never having found "a quiet and intelligent woman" to marry when Mars was fully inhabited, Walter is shocked by the sound of a ringing phone. On the other end is the voice of Genevieve Selsor. Ecstatic, he arranges to meet her and conjures up a beautiful woman with "long dark hair shaking in the wind" and "lips like red peppermints." When he meets her and sees that she in fact has a "round and thick" face with eyes "like two immense eggs stuck into a white mess of bread dough," he endures a painful evening with her before fleeing for a life of solitary survivalism. Though the chapter provides a moment of levity compared to the ruined civilization chapters that follow and close out the book, the humor in "The Silent Towns" is carefully crafted toward nervous-ness. It is in the vein of comedy Donald Hassler identifies in *Comic Tones in Science Fiction: The Art of Compromise with Nature* that "refuse[s] to be tragic and yet [is] filled with pathos because [it] represents *just* survival." The story's humor serves primarily to deromanticize the last-man-on-earth motif: though atomic war may have made Walter Gripp a master of all he surveys, it has also perpetuated and intensified his isolation.

"There Will Come Soft Rains," the novel's penultimate chapter, restores the tone in *The Martian Chronicles* to grimness, depicting the "tomb planet" character of Mars alluded to one chapter earlier in "The Long Years." The "character" in this chapter is an ultramodern home on post–atomic war Earth in 2026, equipped with turn-of-the-twenty-first-century gadgetry. A voice-clock repeats the time of day each minute, and a kitchen ceiling reads off the date. The automatic kitchen cooks breakfast for four; the patio walls open up into bridge tables; the nursery walls glow and animate themselves at children's hour; the beds warm their own sheets; and the tub fills itself with bath water. This technology wastes away mindlessly, however, for "the gods had gone away." This is the wasteland of thermonuclear destruction: the home is "the one house left standing" in a "ruined city" whose "radioactive glow could be seen for miles." The only signs of life (other than the various "small cleaning animals, all rubber and metal") are a dying dog and the evidence of a family vaporized by atomic explosion: "The entire west face of the house was black, save for five places. Here the silhouette in paint of a man mowing a lawn. Here, as in a photograph, a woman bent to pick flowers. Still farther over, their images burned on wood in one titanic instant, a small boy, hands flung into the air; higher up, the image of a thrown ball, and opposite him, a girl, hands raised to catch a ball which never came down." The chapter ends with the house endlessly spinning out its daily mechanical routine to the ghosts of its vaporized inhabitants. It is perhaps the most vivid image Bradbury's cold war novels offer of the synthetic hell man makes for himself from the raw materials of science, technology, and irrationality.

Fahrenheit 451 resumes the examination of precarious existence in an atomic age that Bradbury began in *The Martian Chronicles*. Fire as the omnipotent weapon in *Fahrenheit* finds metaphoric parallels in the notion of the bomb as the omnipotent force in the cold war years. The early tests of the Los Alamos project, for example, paid close attention to the extreme temperatures produced by the fissioning and fusioning of critical elements. J. Robert Oppenheimer, Niels Bohr, and Edward Teller based key decisions in the atomic bomb (and later the hydrogen bomb) designs on the core temperatures created at the moment of detonation. Montag and the Firemen of America, likewise, are ever conscious of the key numeral 451 (the temperature at which books burn), so much so that it is printed on their helmets. The linking of hubris with the attainment of power is evident in both the Los Alamos scientists and the Firemen as well. As the Manhattan Project was drawing to a close, the team of physicists who designed the bomb came to exude a high degree of pride in their mastery of science, but without an attendant sense of responsibility. As Lamont explains, the bomb "represented the climax of an intriguing intellectual match between the scientists and the cosmos. The prospect of solving the bomb's cosmic mysteries, of having their calculations proved correct, seemed far more fascinating and important to the scientists than the prospect of their opening an era obsessed by fear and devoted to the control of those very mysteries." *Fahrenheit 451* opens with Montag similarly blinded by his own perceived importance: "He knew that when he returned to the firehouse, he might wink at himself, a minstrel man, burnt-corked, in the mirror. Later, going to sleep, he would feel the fiery smile still gripped by his face muscles, in the dark. It never went away, that smile, it never ever went away, as long as he remembered." Like the engineers of atomic destruction, the engineer of intellectual destruction feels the successful completion of his goals entitles him to a legitimate smugness. The work of the cold war physicists, in retrospect, also shares something else with Montag, which Donald Watt points out: "Montag's destructive burning . . . is blackening, not enlightening; and it poses a threat to nature."

Fahrenheit 451 also expands on the anxiety over the atomic bomb and fear of a nuclear apocalypse introduced in *Chronicles*. In *Fahrenheit*, Beatty endorses the official government position that, as "custodians of our peace of mind," he and Montag should "let [man] forget there is such a thing as war." Once Montag has decided to turn his back on the firehouse, however, he tries conveying his personal sense of outrage to Mildred at being kept ignorant, hoping to incite a similar concern in her: "How in hell did those bombers get up there every single second of our lives! Why doesn't someone want to talk about it! We've started and won two atomic wars since 1990!" Mildred, however, is perfectly uninspired and breaks off the conversation to wait for the White Clown to enter the TV screen. But Montag's unheeded warning becomes reality; the bombs are dropped once Montag meets up with Granger and the book people, just as they became reality in "There Will Come Soft Rains," and Montag's horrific vision of the bomb's shock wave hitting the building where he imagines Mildred is staying captures a chilling image of his ignorant wife's last instant of life:

> Montag, falling flat, going down, saw or felt, or imagined he saw or felt the walls go dark in Millie's face, heard her screaming, because in the millionth part of time left, she saw her own face reflected there, in a mirror instead of a crystal ball, and it was such a wild empty face, all by itself in the room, touching nothing, starved and eating of itself, that at last she recognized it as her own and looked quickly up at the ceiling as it and the entire structure of the hotel blasted down upon her, carrying her with a million pounds of brick, metal, plaster, and wood, to meet

other people in the hives below, all on their quick way down to
the cellar where the explosion rid itself of them in its own unreasonable way.

Perhaps Bradbury's own sense of fear at a future that must accommodate
atomic weapons had intensified between *The Martian Chronicles*'s publication in 1950 and *Fahrenheit 451*'s completion in 1953; perhaps what David
Mogen identifies as Bradbury's inspiration for the book, Hitler's book
burnings, affords little room for the comic. For whatever reasons, unlike
Chronicles, which intersperses the solemnity of its nuclear aftermath chapters with a bit of lightness in the Walter Gripp story, Fahrenheit sustains a
serious tone to the end of the book, even in its resurrectionist optimism for
the future of the arts.

This optimism for the future—this notion of recivilization—is the
third common element between *The Martian Chronicles* and *Fahrenheit 451*
that has early cold war connections. Given such nihilistic phenomena of the
cold war era as its tendencies toward censorship, its socially paranoid
outlook, and its budding arms race, it may seem a strange period to give rise
to any optimism. However, one of the great ironies of the period was a
peripheral belief that somehow the presence of nuclear arms would, by their
very capacity to bring about ultimate destruction to *all* humans, engender a
very special sort of cautiousness and cooperative spirit in the world hereto-
fore not experienced. Perhaps there was a belief that Hiroshima and
Nagasaki had taught us a big enough lesson in themselves about nuclear cata-
clysm that we as humans would rise above our destructive tendencies and live
more harmoniously. One very prominent figure who espoused this position
was Dr. J. Robert Oppenheimer, the very man who headed the Los Alamos
Manhattan Project. Oppenheimer would emerge as one of the most morally
intriguing characters of the cold war. He was among the first in the scientific
community to encourage restraint, caution, and careful deliberation in all
matters regarding the pursuit of atomic energy. "There is only one future of
atomic explosives that I can regard with any enthusiasm: that they should
never be used in war," he said in a 1946 address before the George Westing-
house Centennial Forum. He also refused to participate in the development
of the hydrogen bomb following Los Alamos, calling such a weapon "the
plague of Thebes" (Rhodes). In one of his most inspired addresses on the
cooperation of art and science, Oppenheimer stated that "Both the man of
science and the man of art live always at the edge of mystery, surrounded by
it; both always, as the measure of their creation, have had to do with the
harmonization of what is new with what is familiar, with the balance between
novelty and synthesis, with the struggle to make partial order in total chaos.

They can, in their work and in their lives, help themselves, help one another, and help all men."

Such a spirit of hope for renewed goodwill among men of all vocations is the optimistic vein through which society is reenvisioned following the atomic devastation of the Earth in "The Million-Year Picnic," the final chapter of *The Martian Chronicles*. Several days in the past, a rocket that had been hidden on Earth during the Great War carried William and Alice Thomas and their children, Timothy, Michael, and Robert, to Mars, presumably for a "picnic." The father admits to his inquisitive sons on this day, however, that the picnic was a front for an escape from life on Earth, where "people get lost in a mechanical wilderness" and "Wars got bigger and bigger and finally killed Earth." The father literally plans a new civilization: he blows up their rocket to avoid discovery by hostile Earthmen; he burns up all the family's printed records of their life on earth; and he now awaits, with his family, "a handful of others who'll land in a few days. Enough to start over. Enough to turn away from all that back on Earth and strike out on a new line." When his son Michael repeats his request to see a "Martian," the father takes his family to the canal and points to their reflections in the water. The book's last line, "The Martians stared back up at them for a long, long silent time from the rippling water," is optimistic without being didactic. It suggests that this new society has in fact already begun, that it is already "making partial order out of total chaos," as Oppenheimer suggests the cold war future needs to do. William F. Touponce believes that it is "an altogether appropriate ending" that "summarizes the experience of the reader, who has seen old illusions and values destroyed only to be replaced with new and vital ones." It also offers an image that invites the reader to extrapolate on the father's vision of "a new line" and trust the will of the colonizers for once.

Bradbury's optimism for a recivilized world is also evident in the conclusion of *Fahrenheit 451*. The seed for an optimistic ending to this dystopian work is actually planted just before the bombs strike. As Montag makes his way across the wilderness, dodging the pursuit of the mechanical hound and the helicopters, he spots the campfire of the book people. His thoughts reflect an epiphany of his transformation from a destroyer of civilization to a builder of it: "[The fire] was not burning. It was *warming*. He saw many hands held to its warmth, hands without arms, hidden in darkness. Above the hands, motionless faces that were only moved and tossed and flickered with firelight. He hadn't known fire could look this way. He had never thought in his life that it could give as well as take." This spirit of giving, of creating from the environment, is emphasized throughout the speeches given by Granger, the leader of the book preservers. In his allusion to the phoenix, which resurrects itself from the ashes of its own pyre,

Granger's words reflect the new Montag, who can now see the life-sustaining properties of fire as well as its destructive powers; hopefully, Granger's words also contain hope for the American response to Hiroshima and Nagasaki: "we've got one damn thing the phoenix never had. We know the damn silly thing we just did. We know all the damn silly things we've done for a thousand years and as long as we know that and always have it around where we can see it, someday we'll stop making the goddamn funeral pyres and jumping in the middle of them." The book ends with Montag rehearsing in his mind a passage from the Book of Revelation, which he says he'll save for the reading at noon. Peter Sisario sees in this ending "a key to Bradbury's hope that 'the healing of nations' can best come about through a rebirth of man's intellect"; Sisario's interpretation of *Fahrenheit*'s ending and Oppenheimer's interpretation of mankind's necessary response to the cold war share a belief in the triumph of the benevolent side of humans.

A fourth theme in Bradbury's cold war novels that has a historical "objective correlative" is the dichotomous nature of the Cold War Man. The Cold War Man is a man antagonized by conflicting allegiances—one to his government, the other to his personal sense of morals and values—who is forced by circumstance to make an ultimate choice between these impulses. This Bradbury character type has roots in cold war political tensions.

During the early cold war years, the United States's international stance frequently wavered between a policy of military supremacy and one of peacetime concessions. One historian notes this phenomenon in the about-face many Americans took toward Roosevelt's role in the shifting of global powers following World War II: ". . . both policy and attitude changed with the Truman administration. The rationale behind Yalta—that a negotiated agreement with the Soviet Union was possible and that the development of mutual trust was the best means to a just and lasting peace—was now rejected in favor of the containment policy and superior military strength" (Theoharis).

These contradictory stances of peace and aggression in our nation's outlook occasionally found expression in the form of a single man during the early cold war. The figure of Dr. J. Robert Oppenheimer again becomes relevant. Though primarily remembered for his contribution to physics, Oppenheimer also had strong leanings toward the humanities; as a youth and in his years as a Harvard undergraduate, he developed a range of literary interests from the Greek classicists to Donne to Omar Khayyam. David Halberstam observes, "To some he seemed the divided man—part creator of the most dangerous weapon in history—part the romantic innocent searching for some inner spiritual truth." For a government-employed physicist, however, this "division" would turn out to be something of a tragic flaw in the cold war years. When Oppenheimer would have no part of the U.S. government's decision to pursue the hydrogen bomb in its initial phase of the arms race with the Soviets, the government began an inquiry into his past. It was "determined" in June of 1954 that Oppenheimer was guilty of Communist associations that jeopardized national security. He was then stripped of his government security clearance, and his service with the Atomic Energy Commission terminated. Thus, in Oppenheimer was a man whose pacifistic sympathies eventually triumphed over his capacity for aggression—and in the early cold war years he was punished for it.

The Oppenheimer figure finds interesting parallels in Bradbury's cold war novels. In "—And the Moon Be Still as Bright" in *The Martian Chronicles*, Spender is torn between the need to serve his Earth-based government (in his participation with the expedition crew on Mars) and the deep personal need to preserve the remains of the native Martian culture, which he believes is threatened by the very kind of expedition he is serving: "When I got up here I felt I was not only free of [Earth's] so-called culture, I felt I was free of their ethics and their customs. I'm out of their frame of reference, I thought. All I have to do is *kill you all off* and *live my own life*" (emphasis added). Spender's surrender to the personal impulse to defend Mars from Earth corruption over the impulse to follow the government-entrusted group leads to his death. Wilder is forced to shoot Spender when he threatens more killings, and his death-image symbolically reinforces his divided self: "Spender lay there, his hands clasped, one around the gun, the other around the silver book that glittered in the sun." The gun, which is entrusted to him as a member of the expedition and the book, which he found in his walks through the Martian ruins, emblematize Spender's divided allegiances. The image is curiously akin to the image Lansing Lamont provides of Oppenheimer's dichotomous self: "With balanced equanimity he could minister to a turtle and select the target cities for the first atomic massacres." Wilder also exudes characteristics of the dichotomous Cold War Man. The captain's sympathies toward the arts and toward Spender's appreciation of them lead him to bury Spender with an aesthetic touch. Finding a Martian sarcophagus, Wilder has the crew "put Spender into a silver case with waxes and wines which were ten thousand years old, his hands folded on his chest." The scene immediately changes from Spender's ornate sarcophagus to the captain's catching Parkhill in one of the dead cities and knocking his teeth out for shooting at the Martian towers. Wilder's coexistent propensity for violence and aesthetic sensibilities mark his dichotomous cold war sides as well. Stendahl in "Usher II" further reflects both sides of this Cold War Man. He possesses the aesthetic appreciation of a literature devotee, a man with an architectural vision of Usher II, specifying to Bigelow the need for colors precisely "desolate and terrible," for walls that are "bleak," for tarn that is "black and lurid," for sedge that is "gray and ebon." Yet this same man furnishes his home with all of Poe's macabre instruments of death: an ape that strangles humans, a razor-sharp pendulum, a coffin for the nailing up of a live woman, and bricks and mortar for sealing up a live victim.

The dichotomous Cold War Man theme is again treated in *Fahrenheit 451*. Both Montag and Beatty are simultaneously capable of the destructive and appreciative of the artistic. As Donald Watt remarks of Montag, "Burning as constructive energy, and burning as apocalyptic catastrophe, are the symbolic poles of Bradbury's novel." Montag's divided self is clearly displayed by Bradbury at moments when his character is being influenced by the intellectually stimulating presences of Clarisse and Faber. Early in the book, when Montag is just beginning to wrestle with his identity as a fireman, Clarisse tells him that being a fireman "just doesn't seem right for you, somehow." Immediately Bradbury tells us that Montag "felt his body divide itself into a hotness and a coldness, a softness and a hardness, a trembling and a not trembling, the two halves grinding one upon the other." Later, after offering his services to Faber and his group, Montag considers the shiftings of his own character that he has been feeling in his conflicting allegiances: "Now he knew that he was two people, that he was, above all, Montag, who knew nothing, who did not even know himself a fool, but only suspected it. And he knew that he was also the old man who talked to him and talked to him as the train was sucked from one end of the night city to the other." Fire Chief Beatty also suggests aspects of the Cold War Man. In spite of his wearing the role of the Official State Majority Leader as the fire chief and relentlessly burning every book at every alarm, Beatty acknowledges that he knows the history of Nicholas Ridley, the man burned at the stake alluded to by the woman who ignites her own home. He gives Montag the reply that most fire captains are "full of bits and pieces"; however, when he later warns Montag against succumbing to the "itch" to read that every fireman gets "at least once in his career," he further adds an ambiguous disclosure: "Oh, to *scratch* that itch, eh? Well, Montag, take my word for it, I've had to read a few in my time to know what I was about, and the books say *nothing!* Nothing you can teach or believe." Though Beatty has an alibi for having some knowledge of literature, Bradbury urges us to question just what Beatty may *not* be telling us. Montag's later certainty over Beatty's desire to die at Montag's hands raises even more questions about Beatty's commitment to the destructive half of his duality.

Through *The Martian Chronicles* and *Fahrenheit 451*, Ray Bradbury has created a microcosm of early cold war tensions. Though the reader will perceive a degree of Bradbury's sociopolitical concerns from a reading of either novel, it is only through the reading of both as companion pieces that his full cold war vision emerges. From the perspective that America has wrestled itself free of the extremism of the McCarthyists and, thus far, has escaped nuclear war as well, Bradbury's cold war novels may have indeed contributed to the "prevention" of futures with cold war trappings.

Chronology

1920   Ray Bradbury born August 22 in Waukegan, Illinois. He is the third son of Leonard Spaulding Bradbury, an electrical lineman, and Esther Marie Moberg Bradbury, a native-born Swede. His twin brothers, Leonard and Samuel, had been born in 1916; Samuel died in 1918.

1926   A sister, Elizabeth, is born; the family moves to Tucson, Arizona, in the fall.

1927   Elizabeth dies of pneumonia and the family returns to Waukegan in May.

1928   Discovers science fiction in *Amazing Stories.*

1931   Writes first stories on butcher paper.

1932   Leonard Bradbury is laid off from his job as a telephone lineman, and the family moves back to Tucson; Ray performs as an amateur magician at Oddfellows Hall and American Legion; reads comics to children on radio station KGAR.

1933   Family returns to Waukegan; Ray sees Century of Progress exhibit at Chicago World's Fair.

1934   Seeking employment, father moves family to Los Angeles where
        Ray works as "live audience" for the Burns and Allen radio show.

1937   Acts as scriptwriter, producer, and director of the *Roman Review*
        at Los Angeles High School; joins the Los Angeles Science
        Fiction League.

1938   Graduates from high school; first short story, "Hollerbochen's
        Dilemma," published in *Imagination!*

1939   Publishes his own fan magazine, *Futuria Fantasia*; attends World
        Science Fiction Convention in New York; joins actress Laraine
        Day's drama group, the Wilshire Players Guild; sells newspapers
        on Los Angeles street corner, a job he keeps until 1942.

1940   "It's Not the Heat It's the Hu . . ." published in *Rob Wagner's
        Script Magazine* on November 2.

1941   Participates in Robert Heinlein's weekly writing class;
        "Pendulum," co-authored with Henry Hasse, published in *Super
        Science Stories*.

1942   Begins earning $20 a week writing short stories and decides to
        quit selling newpapers to write full-time; his story "The Lake"
        is the first to exhibit his distinctive style.

1945   Begins publishing in "slick" magazines; travels to Mexico; "The
        Big Black and White Game" included in *Best American Short
        Stories*.

1947   Marries Marguerite McClure; publishes first book, *Dark
        Carnival*; "Homecoming" wins O. Henry Award and is published
        in *Prize Stories of 1947*; becomes client of literary agent Don
        Congdon.

1948   "Powerhouse" wins O. Henry Award; "I See You Never" selected
        for *Best American Short Stories 1948*.

1949   Selected as "best author of 1949" for fantasy and science fiction
        by the National Fantasy Fan Federation; first daughter born.

1950   *The Martian Chronicles* published; republished in London as *The Silver Locusts*, 1951.

1951   *The Illustrated Man* published; republished London, 1952; second daughter born.

1952   Writes *It Came from Outer Space*; "The Other Foot" published in *Best American Short Stories*.

1953   *The Golden Apples of the Sun* and *Fahrenheit 451* published; travels to Ireland, stays six months to write screenplay for John Huston's *Moby Dick*; wins Benjamin Franklin Award for year's best short story published in a popular magazine.

1954   Awarded $1,000 from American Academy of Arts and Letters for contributions to American literature.

1955   *Switch on the Night*, a children's book, published; *The October Country* published; third daughter born.

1956   *Dandelion Wine* and *Sun and Shadow* published. Leonard Bradbury dies.

1958   Fourth daughter born.

1959   *A Medicine for Melancholy* published; "The Day It Rained Forever" is selected for *Best American Short Stories*.

1962   *Something Wicked This Way Comes, The Small Assassin*, and *R Is for Rocket* published.

1963   Receives Academy Award nomination for *Icarus Montgolfier Wright*; publishes first collection of drama, *The Anthem Sprinters and Other Antics*.

1964   *The Machineries of Joy: Short Stories* and *The Pedestrian* published; *American Journey*, his film history of the nation, opens at the New York World's Fair; produces *The World of Ray Bradbury* at the Coronet Theatre, Los Angeles.

1965   Produces *The Wonderful Ice Cream Suit* in Los Angeles; *The World of Ray Bradbury* has brief, unsuccessful run in New York. "The Other Foot" selected for *Fifty Best American Short Stories: 1915–1965*. *The Autumn People* published by Ballantine; *The Vintage Bradbury* published by Random House.

1966   Francois Truffaut's movie *Fahrenheit 451* released; *Twice Twenty-Two*, *Tomorrow Midnight* and *S Is for Space* published; Esther Moberg Bradbury dies.

1967   *Dandelion Wine* produced as musical drama at Lincoln Center; *The Anthem Sprinters*, a collection of Irish plays, produced at Beverly Hills Playhouse.

1968   Wins Aviation-Space Writers Association award for "An Impatient Gulliver Above Our Roots," a science article published in *Life Magazine*.

1969   Film version of *The Illustrated Man* released; *I Sing the Body Electric! Stories* published; *Christus Apollo*, a cantata, performed at UCLA.

1970   "Mars Is Heaven!" selected for the Science Fiction Hall of Fame by the Science Fiction Writers of America.

1972   *The Wonderful Ice Cream Suit and Other Plays* and *The Halloween Tree* published; *Madrigals for the Space Age*, for Mixed Chorus and Narrator with Piano Accompaniment, published.

1973   *When Elephants Last in the Dooryard Bloomed*, Bradbury's first collection of poetry, published.

1975   *Pillar of Fire and Other Plays* published.

1976   *Long After Midnight* published.

1977   *Where Robot Mice and Robot Men Run Round in Robot Towns*, a collection of poetry, published; receives Life Achievement Award at the World Fantasy Convention.

1980   *The Stories of Ray Bradbury* and "The Last Circus and The Electrocution" published; receives Gandolf Award as "Grand Master" at the Hugo Award Ceremonies.

1981   *The Haunted Computer and the Android Pope*, a collection of poetry, published.

1982   *The Complete Poems of Ray Bradbury* and *The Love Affair* published.

1983   *Dinosaur Tales* published.

1984   Film version of *Something Wicked This Way Comes*, screenplay by Bradbury, released; *Forever and the Earth: Radio Dramatization* published. A collection of early mystery stories, *A Memory of Murder*, published; receives Jules Verne Award; receives Valentine Davies Award from the Writers Guild of America for his work in films.

1985   *Death Is a Lonely Business* published.

1987   *Death Has Lost Its Charm For Me*, poems, published.

1988   *The Toynbee Convector*, a collection of stories, published.

1989   *The Climate of Palettes* published.

1990   Published *The Day It Rained Forever* (a musical), *A Graveyard for Lunatics*, (a novel), *Another Tale of Two Cities*, (a novel), *Zen and the Art of Writing*, (a collection of essays on the art and craft of writing).

1991   *Yestermorrow: Obvious Answers to Impossible Futures*, essays, published.

1992   *Green Shadows, White Whale*, a novel, published.

1993   "The Stars," a poem, published.

1996   *Quicker Than the Eye*, a collection of stories, published.

1997   *Driving Blind*, a collection of stories; two poems, "Dogs Think that Every Day is Christmas" and "With Cat for Comforter" published.

Contributors

HAROLD BLOOM is Sterling Professor of the Humanities at Yale University and Henry W. and Albert A. Berg Professor of English at the New York University Graduate School. He is the author of over 20 books, including *Shelley's Mythmaking* (1959), *The Visionary Company* (1961), *Blake's Apocalypse* (1963), *Yeats* (1970), *A Map of Misreading* (1975), *Kabbalah and Criticism* (1975), *Agon: Toward a Theory of Revisionism* (1982), *The American Religion* (1992), *The Western Canon* (1994), and *Omens of Millennium: The Gnosis of Angels, Dreams, and Resurrection* (1996). *The Anxiety of Influence* (1973) sets forth Professor Bloom's provocative theory of the literary relationships between the great writers and their predecessors. His most recent books include *Shakespeare: The Invention of the Human*, a 1998 National Book Award finalist, and *How to Read and Why*, which was published in 2000. In 1999, Professor Bloom received the prestigious American Academy of Arts and Letters Gold Medal for Criticism.

DAMON KNIGHT is a distinguished writer, editor, and critic of science fiction. He is the former editor of *Orbit*, an influential series of hardcover anthologies of science fiction published between 1966 and 1980, as well as the author of numerous science-fiction novels, including *A for Anything* (reissued in 1998 by Cascade Mountain Publishing), *Humpty Dumpty: An Oval* (1996), *First Contact* (1978), and *The Rithian Terror* (1965). A revised third edition of his essay collection *In Search of Wonder: Essays on Modern Science Fiction* appeared in 1999.

WAYNE L. JOHNSON is the author of *Ray Bradbury* (1980). He has contributed articles and essays to numerous journals, and contributed to the collection *Critical Encounters: Writers and Themes in Science Fiction* (1978).

WILLIAM F. TOUPONCE has written several critical articles on the works of Ray Bradbury and has recently written for the journal *Children's Literature*.

HAZEL PIERCE teaches at Kearney State College, Kearney, Nebraska. She is a contributor to *Isaac Asimov* in the WRITERS OF THE 21ST CENTURY series and has written book reviews for the Science Fiction Research Association newsletter.

LAHNA DISKIN is co-editor of the anthology *Courage*, and co-author and editor of *Short Story*, which contains literature units for high school students. As a member of the National Council of Teachers of English, she has served as speaker and consultant at numerous conferences and conventions.

GARY K. WOLFE is associate professor of humanities at Roosevelt University in Chicago. He has participated in Modern Language Association seminars on science fiction and mythology and has published essays on popular literature, film, and adult education, as well as on science fiction.

KEVIN HOSKINSON is associate professor of developmental English at Lorain County Community College in Elyria, Ohio. His teaching and scholarly research focus upon 20th century American literature and Irish drama.

Bibliography

Amis, Kingsley. *New Maps of Hell: A Survey of Science Fiction*. New York: Arno, 1975.

Attebery, Brian. *The Fantastic Tradition in American Literature from Irving to LeGuin*. Bloomington: Indiana University Press, 1980.

Cuppy, Will. "Review of *Dark Carnival*." *New York Herald Tribune Books* (25 May 1947): 30.

Davidson, Avram. "Review of *Something Wicked This Way Comes*." *Magazine of Fantasy and Science Fiction* 25 (July 1963): 105–6.

Dziemianowicz, Stefan. "Back to the Future." *Necrofile* 9 (Summer 1993): 24.

Greenberg, Martin Harry, and Joseph D. Olander, eds. *Ray Bradbury*. New York: Taplinger, 1980.

Hamblin, Charles F. "Bradbury's *Fahrenheit 451* in the Classroom." *English Journal* 57 (September 1968): pp. 818–19.

Hienger, Jorg. "The Uncanny and Science Fiction," translated by Elsa Schneider. *Science Fiction Studies* 6 (1979): 144–52.

Huntington, John. "Utopian and Anti-Utopian Logic: H. G. Wells and His Successors." *Science-Fiction Studies* 9 (1982): 122–46.

Isherwood, Christopher. "Christopher Isherwood Reviews *The Martian Chronicles*." *Tomorrow* (October 1950): 56–58.

Jacobs, Robert. "Interview with Ray Bradbury." *The Writer's Digest* 55 (February 1976): 18–25.

King, Stephen. *Danse Macabre*. New York: Everest House, 1981.

Kirk, Russell. *Enemies of Permanent Things*. New Rochelle, N.Y.: Arlington House, 1969.

Mogen, David. *Ray Bradbury*. Boston: Twayne, 1986.

Moskowitz, Sam. *Seekers of Tomorrow, Masters of Modern Science Fiction*. New York: Ballantine, 1967.

Nolan, William F. *The Bradbury Companion: A Life and Career History, Photolog, and Comprehensive Checklist of Writings With Facsimiles From Ray Bradbury's Unpublished and Uncollected Work in All Media*. Detroit: Gale Research, 1975.

Slusser, George Edgar. *The Bradbury Chronicles*. San Bernardino, Calif.: Borgo Press, 1977.

Warrick, Patricia S., and Martin Harry Greenberg, eds. *The New Awareness: Religion Through Science Fiction*. New York: Delacorte Press, 1975.

Acknowledgments

"When I Was in Knee Pants: Ray Bradbury" by Damon Knight. From *In Search of Wonder: Essays on Modern Science Fiction.* © 1956, 1967 by Damon Knight. Reprinted with permission.

"The Invasion Stories of Ray Bradbury" by Wayne L. Johnson. From *Critical Encounters: Writers and Themes in Science Fiction*, Dick Riley, ed. © 1978 by Frederick Ungar Publishing Co., Inc. Reprinted with permission.

"Dusk in the Robot Museums: The Rebirth of Imagination" by Ray Bradbury. From *MOSAIC* 13, no. 3–4 (Spring–Summer 1980; special issue, titled *Other Worlds: Fantasy and Science Fiction Since 1939*, John J. Teunissen, ed.): v–x. © 1980 by the University of Manitoba. Reprinted with permission.

"*The Martian Chronicles* and Other Mars Stories" by Wayne L. Johnson. From *Ray Bradbury.* © 1980 by Frederick Ungar Publishing Co., Inc. Reprinted with permission.

"The Existential Fabulous: A Reading of Ray Bradbury's 'The Golden Apples of the Sun'" by William F. Touponce. From *MOSAIC* 13, no. 3–4 (Spring–Summer 1980; special issue, titled *Other Worlds: Fantasy and Science Fiction Since 1939*, John J. Teunissen, ed): 203–17. © 1980 by the University of Manitoba. Reprinted with permission.

"Ray Bradbury and the Gothic Tradition" by Hazel Pierce. From *Ray Bradbury*, Martin Harry Greenberg and Joseph D. Olander, eds. © 1980 by Martin Harry Greenberg and Joseph D. Olander. Reprinted with permission.

"Bradbury on Children" by Lahna Diskin. From *Ray Bradbury*, Martin Harry Greenberg and Joseph D. Olander, eds. © 1980 by Martin Harry Greenberg and Joseph D. Olander. Reprinted with permission.

"The Frontier Myth in Ray Bradbury" by Gary K. Wolfe. From *Ray Bradbury*, Martin Harry Greenberg and Joseph D. Olander, eds. © 1980 by Martin Harry Greenberg and Joseph D. Olander. Reprinted with permission.

"*The Martian Chronicles* and *Fahrenheit 451:* Ray Bradbury's Cold War Novels" by Kevin Hoskinson. From *Extrapolation* 36, no. 4. (Winter 1995): 347–57. © 1995 by The Kent State University Press. Reprinted with permission.

Index